The Grand Design - II
Reflections of a soul/oversoul

PADDY MCMAHON

Sooner or later questions such as "Who and/or what am I? Where did I come from? How can I find meaning in my life? How can I reduce the pain of self-realisation? What will happen to me when I die?" begin to niggle at each of us. This book provides answers that come from a spirit being named SHEBAKA.

The Grand Design books, of which there are five volumes, explore life in all its aspects both in the physical world and in spirit. Inter alia, they explain how we came to inhabit physical bodies and what happens to us when we die; and they provide facts, concepts and suggestions designed to help us, in cooperation with our guides/guardian angels if we so wish, to find ever increasing happiness and fulfilment in our expression.

CONTENTS

PREFACE

This is the second volume of a series of books which I'm writing, I believe, in association with a spirit being, known to me as Shebaka. My first conscious communication with Shebaka took place in 1981. I recorded the initial communications in date order as they happened without having any intention of publishing them. Putting in the dates seemed to me to be significant - at least for myself - in that they signposted my own evolution, my capacity to receive, understand and accept the information and concepts being transmitted to me. My communication with Shebaka is not an automatic process; I don't just sit and write down words and sentences as if they are being dictated to me. Many times I have wished that it (the communication) would be automatic - not only because that would be so much easier for me but also because there would be no risk that I would misinterpret or distort the communication, which would make the whole operation a meaningless exercise. The communication works with me by way of impressions which I have to fit into my own language structure. The effect is that the format of the writing bears my own style and my own way of expressing myself and, indeed, suffers from the limitations of my own vocabulary. At the same time, I trust and believe that I have conveyed accurately the essence of what has been transmitted to me and in the process illuminated and, I hope, eliminated much of my own unawareness - which, I understand, is partly why I'm not functioning as just an automatic channel for Shebaka.

As I explained in the preface to the first volume, I approached its publication with a lot of trepidation which was, of course, a clear indication of how much I was still afflicted by egotism since my hesitancy was due not to any doubts about the validity of the material contained in the book but to my own fears about what it would do to

1

my image in the eyes of people who knew me. Even though I comforted myself with the knowledge that no two people could hold exactly the same image of anybody and that therefore there can be no such thing as a consistent or uniform public image of any person (with public meaning any number greater than one), yet I recoiled from my expectation that the nature of the book would inevitably categorise me in a particular way.

During the intervening period since the publication of the first book I think (l hope!) that I have shed a lot of the egotism. In any case, publication of this volume doesn't worry me from the point of view of coauthorship of it. It has been a great help, of course, that reaction to the first book (at least the reaction conveyed to me) has been most encouraging with comments from many people about how much it changed and expanded their whole approach to life. I'd have felt it worthwhile writing the book even if only one person apart from myself had felt that. I have also been somewhat surprised that people who hold what I would regard as rigidly orthodox beliefs have apparently found at least some parts of the book interesting and stimulating. At this stage, of course, the limited circulation of the book has more or less ensured that the people who would be inclined to read it would be, to some extent at least, attuned, even unconsciously, to the material in it.

Some of the sessions in this book are extensions or e1aborations of sessions in the first book. I suspect that some people who could broadly accept the first book will find some of the statements in this book hard to take; they (the statements) are certainly in conflict with orthodox religious teaching. I'd prefer if that weren't so. After all, one may well ask who am I to set myself up against the accumulated wisdom of many minds and many centuries. I can only answer that I don't wish to set myself up against anybody or against any teaching. I don't want to be a rebel or a heretic or a martyr or a representative of any cause or any cult.

In whatever ways I can I want to help people to be themselves. If I didn't believe that the material in the book would do that I think I'd be very foolish indeed to publish it. I have choices, of course - play safe or put my toe in the water. I choose the latter - and let the ripples go where they will. In any case, any reader also has choices -

to accept or to reject.

In the long run I have a feeling that orthodoxy and awareness don't - probably can't - coexist. Orthodoxy may perhaps be likened to the stumbling steps of childhood (although very definitely not to the sense of wonder in childhood). By its nature orthodoxy imposes limitations of consciousness while the free spirit knows no limitation.

In publishing this series of books I haven't initially used my surname, which is McMahon, for two reasons: (a) because in my earlier years I had understood that my given names were Patrick Francis until I noticed that there was no Francis on my birth certificate and I thought that having got used to the name I'd like to take it back, and (b) I felt that dropping the surname would protect my privacy, particularly where the telephone was concerned, to some extent. Whatever name I use doesn't seem to me to have any significance since it's the material that's in the books that's important, but I mention the matter in case I might inadvertently convey an impression that I wish to avoid my responsibility for the books. Of course, I fully acknowledge and accept that responsibility.

I hope that readers will be helped, as I have been, to see and feel that life based on the simplicity, and yet profundity, of love holds infinitely interesting and joyful possibilities. Indeed it occurs to me that I should have used the word "certainties" instead of "possibilities".

Paddy McMahon
April, 1991.

CONSCIOUS AND SUBCONSCIOUS – III

15th – 17th April, 1982: It is not an uncommon experience for people to become mentally unhinged and lose the power of coherent thought at some stage of their lives. What happens to them if they die in that state?

Life is, of course, a continuity. The mind doesn't undergo a miraculous transformation on the death of the body. All that happens is that it sheds its physical cage and is no longer subject to physical limitations.

I would define mental stability or sanity as a condition in which the conscious prevails over the subconscious and insanity as a condition in which the subconscious prevails over the conscious.

Many people operate in a 50-50 state between the conscious and subconscious. This is a precarious state where a small tilt towards the subconscious will give it a controlling influence. Periods of depression, for example, or worry, or emotional outbursts, or religious fanaticism, or regular immoderate consumption of alcohol or drugs, or sexual obsessiveness, or any similar conditions, can easily upset the delicate balance between the conscious and the subconscious or, if you like, between sanity and insanity.

Even though most people experience periods of insanity during their lives they are usually able to get back to at least a 50-50 state. But in some cases the subconscious takes over apparently permanent control and they are no longer able to communicate rationally.

The explanation in all cases comes back to free will. Souls perform certain activities which bring consequences. When they reach the

4

second stage they have been brought up to a level of awareness where the mind is more than 50% conscious - in other words, the conscious is in control. By the use of their free will they either increase that percentage or decrease it.

The struggle between the conscious and the subconscious continues through the agency of the free will. Usually a soul is ready to enter the third stage when the balance is about 80:20 in favour of the conscious. At the fourth stage the proportion of subconscious influence remaining is usually in the range of 5% to 10% and certainly not more than 10%.

A soul which lapses into insanity and leaves its physical body in that state may remain in it for some time; the length of time depends on the way it responds to the help being provided for it. This help takes many forms which are all geared towards building on the awareness which it already has and reducing the extent of its subconsciousness.

Some forms of apparent insanity on earth are caused by brain damage. I say apparent insanity since the brain is the physical mechanism which the mind uses for its earth existence and therefore is no longer operative when the body dies. What happens in such cases is rather like an extended sleep condition; once the mind is free of the body it resumes its former state.

There is no need to be depressed about the fact that a soul may remain in a state of insanity for some time after the death of its body. As you know, conditions of insanity are often successfully or partially successfully treated on earth by healing methods, including shock treatment. (I mention shock treatment because some brain damage may result from it but this does not necessarily affect the mind in an adverse way - any more than, say, damage to an arm or a leg.) If spirit beings can help each other on earth they can also do so when they are no longer on earth. (And, of course, psychiatrists have guides too!)

Once the subconscious is eliminated a soul has regained its former state of full awareness. At all the stages of development up to and including the sixth a certain element of subconscious influence exists. In some of the states of the first stage the element of awareness remaining in the mind is virtually non-existent - a fraction of 1%. Gradually through the states of the first stage the awareness is increased to where the soul is conscious of itself as an entity and is therefore ready for the second stage at which point the conscious is in control, even if only marginally so, and free will is again operative.

DREAMS; MEMORY

19th – 25th April: In our first book I touched on dreams a little. I feel it would be worthwhile to elaborate somewhat on the subject. First I will go back over what I already said and then expand on that. I won't confine myself to dreams exclusively as I will have to go into other related areas in order to present as clear a picture as I can.

Dreams may be a product of the subconscious, or a means used by guides to convey guidance, or recollections of astral travelling. If they appear to be a jumble of nonsense they are more than likely a product of the subconscious, if they seem to be framed in symbolical terms they are probably messages from guides, and if they seem to be straightforward, that is direct communication with souls or visits to places, they are likely to be recollections of astral travelling.

As I outlined earlier, all life on earth - stationary and non-stationary - is animated by spirit (God): within that, non-stationary or mobile physical life is animated by parts of individual souls (non-humans) and individual souls (humans). The motive force in non-stationary life is the mind (soul); once that leaves the body it (the body) has no mobility although it may still have life - like a person in a coma. A baby's body in its mother's womb has life but it doesn't have mobility until the soul decides to go into the body.

The soul is, of course, non-material and the body is material. How does the material confine the non-material? You will remember that I said that the brain was the physical mechanism used by the mind during its earth experience. The mind stays with the brain in the head; it has to or the body would cease to function in a mobile way.

The grand design is most accommodating. It provides that the body needs sleep in order to sustain it and this allows the soul freedom from limitation, usually for a number of hours each night. It may not wish to use its freedom to engage in what is known as astral travelling but, as a general rule, most souls leave their bodies every night or whenever the bodies take their regular sleep.

The soul, being non-material, is not inhibited by a material cage, so it has no difficulty in leaving the body. However, it is always conscious that the body may be subject to sudden awakening so it links itself to the brain and is able to return from its travels in an instant if necessary. Most people will have experienced waking up with a start at least once in their lives; what has probably happened is that the soul has returned too quickly and reactivated the brain suddenly.

What does the soul do on its travels? It may go to some place which means a lot to it; or may meet with friends or relatives who are now in spirit; or it may meet other souls who are also astral travelling in order, say, to clear up a misunderstanding or to solve a problem or just to have a chat (in a manner of speaking!); or it may go to seek advice or guidance from its guided or other spirit sources; or it may just itself drift, enjoying its freedom.

While the body, including the brain, sleeps, the soul is still awake in its conscious and subconscious states. When the body is awake it is generally occupied in doing something involving at least a certain amount of concentration. When the body is asleep, however, there is no rein on the subconscious mind. The letting loose of its stored-up fears and guilts and anxieties causes disturbed or nonsensical dreams or nightmares.

If the soul can through astral travelling communicate direct with spirit, including its guides, why is it necessary for guides to send messages through symbolical dreams? Even if a soul may have lost contact with its guides why can't the guides just approach it and say something like ¬– 'Remember us?' – and take it from there? This goes back to the end of our first book when I explained why it was thought best that guidance should be unobtrusive, indeed why it was necessary that it should be. Unless a soul seeks them out the guides will not impose themselves on it. At the same time they have undertaken to help the soul achieve its life purpose in whatever way they can so if it doesn't approach them directly they will seek to help indirectly. The use of symbols in dreams is one way because they may excite curiosity and thus questions and answers opening up a path to increased awareness. Needless to say, though, direct communication is much simpler and better.

Why can't people remember dreams or astral travelling more easily? My definition of memory was that it was the mind's way of remembering things. It follows from that that memory does not cease with the death of the body in the same way as the brain does. It would also be logical to assume that if life is a continuity stretching back through aeons each person would have memories of events beyond his present lifetime. Yet most people don't have such memories.

The explanation is that the grand designers thought it best that souls should be given repeated opportunities to make fresh starts along the road to awareness. This was the origin of memory as you know it. In its aware state the mind has access to all knowledge and has no need of memory. Because unawareness happened some device had to be found which would both protect the mind from knowledge about itself and others, which would hinder its progress, and also help to bring to its attention matters which were necessary for its development. In other words, memory is a screen for the mind and is no longer operative once the mind regains its full awareness.

Broadly speaking, memory works in such a way that the mind remembers whatever it needs to remember at any given time. It is flexible and self-adjusting and during earth lives it works through the brain (as one would expect since it is intricately linked with the mind). Accordingly, brain damage will obscure the memory during an earth life but, like the mind, it will be restored to its former state after the death of the body.

If memory acts as a screen for the mind, why do people remember, say, nightmares or nonsensical dreams? What happens is rather like the soul getting back into the body and reactivating the brain too suddenly. The subconscious in control runs riot and in the process reactivates the brain. The memory is temporarily at the mercy of the subconscious until the conscious part of the mind asserts itself and assumes control. Dreams fade quickly from the memory once the conscious mind takes over. Making special effort to remember dreams doesn't help awareness and in practice probably hinders it. The conscious mind will remember without effort whatever it needs to remember.

I realise that the whole business about mind and memory may seem rather complicated at first sight so I'll try to encapsulate it in a final paragraph. The mind and the soul are one. In the case of the 1% who lost awareness the mind is temporarily divided into conscious and subconscious. The grand design of the 99% (the Father) is aimed at getting rid of the subconscious. As a means of helping to achieve that aim the faculty of memory was introduced to screen the conscious mind from the effects of its subconscious, as well as from the burden of other extraneous material, which might make the way back to full awareness too difficult for it.

RELIGION

27th April – 1st May: I deliberately refrained from saying very much about religion in our first book because it's an emotive subject and I would wish that anything I have to say would tend to eliminate emotions rather than encourage them. However, religion is a matter of fundamental interest to souls so I feel that I must discuss it in greater depth.

How did religion come about in the first place? As a result of the fall from awareness souls lost sight of their greatness as parts of God. Under the grand design help was made available to them in many different ways, notably inspiration and the example of advanced souls. In due course souls began to realise that it was possible to get help from higher sources. In so called pagan times there were many gods who were worshipped as higher beings by people forming themselves into groups. Joyful happenings came to be seen as signs of favour on the part of a god or gods and occasions of sorrow were marks of godly displeasure which called for placatory offerings or sacrifices. Thus the ethos of reward and punishment grew - reward for behaviour thought to be pleasing to the gods and punishment for behaviour thought to be offensive to them.

Later religions concentrated their worship on one god, but the concept of a higher being who dispensed reward and punishment remained and still remains.

Religions were born out of the felt need for worship of apparently unpredictable and arbitrary higher power(s). From time to time people emerged who considered that a new truth or the whole truth had been revealed to them by God. Others came to share their conviction and in due course organisations were built around them.

Thus the world now has a multiplicity of religions and religious organisations.

All religions play a part in the grand design. Bear in mind that earth and its experiences are there for learning purposes. Religions provide many learning opportunities; for example, cooperative effort, community living, thoughtfulness towards others, respect for others, working towards higher ideals. The fact that there are so many religions is an encouragement of tolerance - although the reverse is often the case - in that it is at least an indication that there may be many versions of truth and many ways to Heaven. Even the very fact that religions or religious beliefs may be occasions of intolerance for some people may in the long run turn out to be a big help to those people; often it is only when extremes of behaviour are reached that self-confrontation can no longer be avoided.

Is any one religion better than another as a stepping-stone to awareness? Not necessarily; they all have their uses and play their parts, as I have said. If a person is born into or becomes a member of a particular religion it is usually because he needs the learning opportunities which that religion can best give him.

The danger with religions is that their members may shelter behind rules and regulations and allow their thinking to be completely conditioned by those rules and regulations. It can be a very comfortable and comforting feeling for a person to have everything mapped out for him; the rules are there, all he has to do is follow them and his future in eternity is assured!
Why should any person born into the security of an established religious framework which gives him a promise of eternal happiness if he lives according to its rules want to, or need to, question the basis of his beliefs?

Each individual soul is unique. It has its own special place in the jig-saw of life. All the parts (souls) fit into the whole and are ineluctably interlinked within the whole but they retain their individuality. Each soul is a combination of feeling and thought. It has to express itself in total balance of feeling and thought in the context of its own individuality before it can be said to have reached full awareness. If it allows any part of its feeling and thought to be done for it by another or others it is not possible for it to express its individuality fully.

What I am saying is that, while religions play their part and are helpful in many positive and negative ways for souls climbing the ladder of awareness, at some stage each soul must come to terms with itself as a unique entity and not just as a member of a particular religious organisation. The life blood of a religious organisation is that its members feel and think in the same way about its teachings; it has to be or it wouldn't survive as an organisation. Obviously there's no room for individuality in more than a limited way in that situation. Accordingly, if a soul wants to continue to climb the ladder it will, when it is ready to do so, abandon membership of organised groupings and find its own unique relationship with, and place within, all life. There are no religions at the seventh stage - in fact, there are no religions beyond the second stage - although there are, of course, former members of religious organisations which served their purpose as a means towards the end of increased awareness.

REINCARNATION – II

4th – 8th May: I have already discussed reincarnation to a certain extent. I don't propose to present arguments trying to prove the truth of my statement that reincarnation is a fact of physical existence on earth. I see no point in trying to prove it; souls will reach their own conclusions about it as they are ready for them. In any event, conclusions reached through proof don't have nearly as much value from an awareness point of view as conclusions reached through reason or, ideally, through inner *knowing*.

For anybody who accepts that reincarnation is a fact I would like to elaborate a little on what I already said. In the early stages of human existence a life-span was generally much longer than it is now; it averaged about 500 years. As things evolved with free will expressing itself in many different ways the grand design kept adjusting itself to accommodate the changing conditions. Because the lifestyles of many led to a diminution of their awareness the application of effective corrective measures became difficult - the grand designers felt that this could more successfully be done with shorter repeated physical lives by which means they hoped that tendencies established in one would not be too firmly entrenched to be offset in another. From its beginning earth was designed as a vehicle by which awareness would be increased but it was not originally a part of the grand design that there should be repeated human existences on earth. As with the initial fall from awareness, shorter physical life-spans accompanied by opportunities for reincarnation were a counterbalancing result of the ways in which free will continued to express itself.

Reincarnation, then, represents a stage of evolution in the grand design. The increasing world population is largely a consequence of reincarnation (and also of souls progressing from the first to the second stage).

The purpose of reincarnation is, of course, to give souls repeated opportunities to raise their awareness. Earth provides a wide range of those opportunities. What are the criteria for determining whether one has mastered all the lessons of earth? Essentially these are:

- acceptance of oneness with all life;
- being at one with all life;
- absolute tolerance of others - their opinions, their way of life, how and what they are; total respect for the free will of others;
- acceptance of the continuity and of the spirituality of life (which implies recognition of spiritual being as distinct from physical being – you are a soul with a body not a body with a soul);
- and, most important, total acceptance of one's place in God (a part of God, equal to each other part).

Put like that, they don't seem to be all that much - but they comprehend a lot of turmoil, unfortunately.

Once a soul has acquired these attributes earth has nothing more to offer it - unless it chooses to reincarnate to help others.

GOD – II

11th – 15th May: At this stage I would like to say a little more about God and, in particular, the infinity of God which is such a difficult idea to grasp.

There is no limit to God. It follows that there is no limit to each soul as part of God, that each soul shares in the infinity of God.

Each soul is an infinite part of God; but God is more than the sum of all souls at any given time. God has a capacity for unlimited expression. There is nothing in existence or nothing will ever exist that has not been, or will not be, an expression of God.

I think it's not too difficult to comprehend that God will have no end (which means also, of course, that each soul will have no end). The real mystery about infinity is the no beginning part.

As suggested in an earlier session, if you imagine the earth completely covered by water with no physical boundaries of any kind you can get some tangible concept of infinity. But, of course, water is obviously a physical substance which had a beginning.

Light, in the sense of non-darkness, is another example. Light can be perceived but not seen by the human eye. It's obvious that it's there and when it's there. But, again, light has an apparent beginning.

Reason tells you that somewhere along the line everything must have a source. But reason can't make any deduction as to how the original source came to be there except to say that it must be rather like a recurring decimal - a source has a source has a source indefinitely.

Reason can, however, take us part of the way. How does anything get created? Take a poem, for example. The first thing that happens is that a person gets a feeling that he wants to write a poem about something, then the feeling expresses itself into thought and the poem follows. The feeling comes first, the thought gives expression to the feeling and the act of creation follows. So it is with all creation. Accordingly, the original source must have been a feeling.

But how did the feeling happen? Here, I'm afraid, is the crunch. I don't know the answer. And I can't find out the answer because it is not known. In other words, this is the ultimate question to which there is no answer or the only answer to which can be that the feeling had no beginning.

I realise the implications of what I'm saying. How can I describe God as an infinity without beginning or end if I can't explain how God had no beginning? The best I can do is the following. A soul cannot lose its capacity for feeling. It may lose its awareness of its capacity but not the capacity itself. I feel, therefore I am - eternally. The capacity has not changed - or I should say remains always the same; it is not subject to change. If it is not subject to change it cannot ever not have existed or ever not exist.

I know that this is an incomprehensible idea when considered in the light of a linear time sequence, but if you can conceive of time in the round - an eternal present - it's not so difficult to grasp.

In my earlier description of God I said that, above all, God was love, infinite love. I felt that it was too soon at that stage to provide this development of that description, but I signposted it in my exploration of the meanings of love. As a description of God I like love best within the all-embracing meanings of that word; although a less ambiguous description would be *feeling and all its expressions*.

Now, having arrived at the description of God as feeling and all its expressions, I need to go back to my earlier statement that God is more than the sum of all souls. Does this mean that with each soul forming part of God all souls together still form only part of God? This question embraces the relationship of creation to its creator. If

God is feeling and all its expressions, then God as well as being creator is also creation. So God is all as all is infinitely - in other words, all souls and all their expression infinitely. Feeling continues to express itself eternally in souls as creator(s) and their acts as creation.

In this context, since I took the example of a poem earlier it might be well to consider the relationship of a poem to its creator. Once a poem is written it has its own existence. However, its content is still one with (the mind of) its creator. In a sense it's an extension of him. Even though at some stage it may be destroyed or changed it still exists in a timeless dimension in its creator.

To take another example; the human body is the most common form of creation. While there are physical agents - the father and mother - the design of each human body is the choice of the soul which will require it for a time; effectively each soul creates the body or bodies which it needs for life on earth. Again, the body has its own existence but it also is at one with its creator. Even though it changes through the years until it eventually dies and disintegrates each stage of its existence is in one way or another embedded in the awareness of its creator.

Creation, then, has its own existence, but its existence is essentially not separate from that of its creator - rather in a real way it is contained in it. Thus God is both creator and creation (actual and potential creation), feeling and all its expressions - in one word, love.

FEELING AND EMOTION

17th – 18th May: I have already made a distinction between feeling and emotion; a little elaboration might be helpful.

Feeling is the real mind (soul). Emotion is the subconscious.

Since feeling and emotion are words which are juxtaposed and often regarded as synonymous in daily usage I will define them in my terms in order to clarify why I make a distinction between them.

Suppose you are a parent with, say, a son. You observe him as he lies sleeping. You let the love that's in you for him flow towards him. You are not making any demands on him or in any way disturbing his harmony; you are uniting your harmony with his. That's feeling in action.

But then suppose that you start to think about things that could happen to him. What if he gets very ill and dies? Or has a bad accident? Or grows up to be a drug addict? Or can't find secure employment? Soon you will have allowed your state of harmony to be replaced by nervous tension, anxiety, worry, fear. They are all emotion in action.

The distinction which I make between feeling and emotion is a bit superfluous in the context of common usage of the words, but my purpose in making the distinction is to highlight the influence of the subconscious in what I might call ordinary day-to-day life.

The regaining of full awareness means the elimination of emotion (within my definition of the word) and, accordingly of course, the subconscious. But in the transitional stages how does emotion, while it is still there, relate to God, or feeling and all its expressions? In other words, is emotion an expression of feeling, even though an admittedly defective one? Yes.

To take an example: anger is clearly a lack of harmony and therefore an emotion. If you become angry and abuse or assault somebody you are giving expression to emotion. But you *are* feeling. What's happening is that you are behaving in an unaware manner.

In human terms there are many horrible actions being performed daily by people against people. These actions, horrible though they are, are expressions of emotion which in turn is expression of feeling. They are actions performed by souls who are equal parts of God with their victims. The problem is that they themselves are victims of their own unawareness (" . . . . they know not what they do").

In the end everything comes back to the tragedy of the fall from awareness; all disharmony is a consequence of that. But it happened, so what must be done is to restore the former position rather than to waste time grieving over its loss.

AWARENESS AND NON-AWARENESS

20th – 22nd May: One thing which I hope has become clear from our sessions to date is that God is all-embracing. Bearing that in mind I would remind you of my definition of good and evil as awareness and non-awareness.

The combination of non-awareness and free will has led and still leads souls into all sorts of difficulties. These difficulties can be variously classified as unhappiness, confusion, depression, phobias, obsessions, conflicts, cruelties, barbarities, intolerance, dogmatism, false pride, fanaticism, apathy, arrogance; each one in its own way constitutes a hell on earth or beyond it, or, quite probably, in both situations.

Needless to say, there is no such place as Hell in the sense of a place of eternal punishment for damned souls. Each soul creates its own hell; the hell that it creates on earth may be just as bad as the hell that it creates beyond it.

There has been much lurid presentation of the tortures of Hell.

Like everything else this serves a purpose if only in a negative way. Anything that makes people stop and think about themselves and where they are going can be helpful.

The polarisation of a personal God with hordes of adoring angels and a personal Devil or Satan with legions of ministering devils was a logical consequence of the prevailing concepts of good and evil. Once good and evil were accepted as realities in total opposition to each other it followed that there had to be a personification of all-good, as the source and director of all-good, and a personification of all-evil, as the source and director of all-evil, also in total opposition to each other. In that situation there could never be a reconciliation of the two forces. Both were, and are, seen to be locked in a continuing struggle for new recruits which will only be finally resolved on a Day of Judgment when those who have chosen God will join Him in eternal happiness in Heaven and those who have chosen Satan will share His eternal torment in Hell. In the common delineation of the struggle God, as the personification of all-good, always fights fairly, but Satan, as the personification of all-evil, is prepared to stoop to anything even to representing Himself as God or one of His angels or saints. As a follow-up to this delineation any communication from a spirit source is regarded as suspect - more than likely Satan or one of His minions up to His usual tricks.

As you will find, some will dismiss these writings as the work of Satan. The fact that I have said that there is neither evil nor devil will be represented as being exactly the kind of statement that suits Satan in that it gives Him the freedom of the park, as it were, and people will not be on their guard against Him - although if there were such a Being as Satan, so full of false pride as He is said to be, I doubt if He'd be prepared to agree, for whatever motive, to have Himself and His Kingdom depicted as non-existent. Megalomaniacs are not notable for their self-effacement.

We have gone into this before and there is no way of proving in the context of these writings whether what I'm saying is true or untrue. If it is true much traditional teaching is untrue unless it is seen in symbolical terms rather than as reality. I, and all who are cooperating with me on this venture, think it is time to replace the morality play, illusion, with reality. I am aiming what I'm saying at reason and beyond reason at the *knowing* within each soul. My representation of life is a totally inclusive one or, if you like, a totally non-exclusive one. There is no place in my representation for Satan, all-evil, eternal devils, or eternal Hell. God is all, all is God, and those souls who are not at present aware of that must eventually return to such awareness if they are ever to be truly themselves.

In the meantime some souls, due to the extent of their non-awareness, behave in such a way as to give, or to encourage the giving of, substance to the traditional beliefs about Satan and devils and evil. If their behaviour is recognised for what it is - the result of non-awareness - they will be treated with far more compassion and understanding and more easily helped to see life in a different way. Ultimately, it is not just they who will be helped, it is all souls. The restoration of complete harmony to life is a matter of vital significance for all souls, but especially, of course, for those who, in their unawareness, are most active in promoting disharmony.

HEALING – I

26th May – 5th June: Healing is a basic need for all people in one way or another. Every human being has at some stage had a physical ailment and/or has suffered from mental stress of some kind.

In the widest meaning of the word healing is a daily happening for every soul, giving and receiving. A kind word or a smile is healing; treating others with respect is healing; helping others even in apparently small ways is healing. Easing the pain caused to a child by a cut knee and helping to restore his self-esteem after he has been hurt in a non-physical way are both forms of healing. The more a soul is in harmony with life the more effective its healing vibration will be.

However, the word healing has tended to be taken to mean the curing of illness or disability, physical and mental; in this session I would like to discuss it in that context.

The inequalities in the human scene are highlighted by the vast differences in the conditions under which people are born and live. Some people are physically very frail and seem to have no resistance to infections; others are robust and are generally immune to physical illness. Many people are born with deformities of some kind and many acquire them during physical lifetimes; others don't have any physical defects. The inequalities are so obvious that there is no need to go into them any further - and, of course, they are not confined to physical attributes.

I know I'm going over some ground already covered in earlier sessions but for the sake of clarity I think it is necessary to do so. It would, I suggest, be impossible to explain in any reasonable way how there could be any meaning to life in the face of all its inequalities if there were no continuity to life. So that's the first step. Once continuity of life is accepted the inequalities can be seen in a different light.

The next step has to do with free will. The soul performs certain actions which bring consequences. In order to make progress along the path of awareness it is faced with certain choices, including the possibility of reincarnation.

If the soul chooses to reincarnate it is again faced with choices as to how much progress it hopes to make in one physical lifetime. If it prefers to move in easy stages or if it has reached a level of awareness where it has only a little more to learn from an earth experience it will probably choose a physical body and an environment geared to its needs for that lifetime. On the other hand, if it has many lessons to learn and wishes to try to learn them quickly it will choose a body and/or an environment with many physical limitations.

The key point is that each individual soul chooses its own physical habitat and lifestyle for a particular purpose. The purpose in most cases is ultimately growth in awareness, but it would be a mistake to draw conclusions from any person's circumstances; some souls choose lives of deprivation as a means of helping others, while some souls choose lives of comfort simply because they want that experience. It's a matter of free will.

Now, perhaps, we could look at healing against the background outlined above. The soul chooses a body with, say, a physical limitation such as deafness, possibly for the reason that it wants to develop its capacity for relating to others in a non-judgmental way. It is born into earth as, say, a female baby.

It takes some time for the child's parents to discover that she is deaf. When they do, they use whatever means they can to see if the deafness can be cured. Eventually they are told that it cannot, so they try to live with the situation and to help their daughter to do so also. Yet they are constantly hoping that sometime in some way she will be cured; they pray, perhaps they go on pilgrimages, they seek help from healing agencies other than the traditional medical ones.

Suppose we take some possible outcomes.

In the first the child is not cured of her deafness, eventually learns to accept it and lives a positive and happy life on earth.

In the second the child is again not cured, becomes embittered as a result and allows the bitterness to colour her whole attitude to life which she endures in a continual state of unhappiness.

In the third she is cured by one or other of the healing methods and goes on to live a positive and happy life.

In the fourth she is also cured but finds little meaning in her life.

All the above outcomes must be considered in the light of the girl's purpose. It is likely that in the first she will have achieved that purpose and unlikely that she will have done so in the second. Again in the third outcome she will probably have achieved her purpose, while not doing so in the fourth.

In the second example it is possible that if she had been cured she might have been helped to do better; equally, in the fourth example she might have achieved more had she not been cured.

The conclusion to be drawn, I think, is that healing is neither a good nor a bad thing in itself; it may have positive or negative results. That is why I have already suggested that ideally healing (of a formal kind) should only be undertaken under guidance.

Where does that leave the medical profession and its healing?
Again I say that ideally people should consult their guides before going to a doctor – not alone about whether to go but also about which doctor to attend, if there is a choice. A doctor may achieve successful results with one patient and be unsuccessful with another even though both may have similar ailments. The guides, with the soul's overall life purpose as their concern, will know which type of healing will best help that purpose. For instance, a soul may need spiritual healing rather than physical healing; instead of bodily healing what may be needed is healing designed to help the soul to benefit

spiritually from the particular illness which it has chosen – possibly a psychiatrist or psychologist or psychotherapist or a spiritual healer of some kind would be of more help than a general practitioner.

It is believed by some that if the soul is in tune with its life purpose the body should not succumb to illness of any kind. This is a misunderstanding of the whole design of the earth existence which is to present people with learning experiences in order to help them to increase their awareness. Illness or disability of any kind can be most valuable learning experiences. So can healing or being healed.

Of course, there are many minor illnesses, such as colds, which affect the body. These don't have any significance in the overall scheme of things any more than discomfort which may temporarily be experienced from, say, too much heat or too much cold at a particular time.

In any discussion of illness or disability the question of pain and suffering needs to be explored. Consider, for instance, the sharp pain caused by a toothache. How does the pain arise?

Obviously, the immediate source of the pain is a defective tooth. But if the body were dead there would be no pain even though the tooth's condition wouldn't have changed (for a while!). Neither would the body experience any pain if it were in a coma, or even just asleep. So it can be said that while the body may be an immediate source of pain it doesn't experience pain. In fact, pain (or suffering) can only be experienced by the mind (soul) – in other words, pain is an expression of feeling.

Suppose we take the example of the toothache again. The body, and to be specific, the tooth within the body, is the immediate source of the pain. We have established that the body itself does not experience the pain but rather the mind which controls the body. It is clear that once the body dies the stimulus of the pain is removed and the mind is, of course, no longer affected. But we also know that the pain from the toothache may be eliminated by other means, such as the filling or extraction of the tooth or the use of medicines.

As has already been explained, the brain is the physical mechanism which the mind uses during an earth lifetime. It is the sensory link for the mind, its physical agent. So, while it is true in the real sense that pain can only be experienced by the mind, it is more accurate to say, in so far as physical pain is concerned, that it can only be experienced by the brain. Thus once the brain is rendered inactive – for instance, by means of anesthetics – no pain is experienced.

As a general rule, the higher the level of awareness the less pain and suffering there is (unless they are specifically chosen as a means of helping others – for instance, by example). That can be readily seen to be so in the case of mental stress – obviously, if people can find meaning in their lives much stress will be removed. But how does it apply to physical pain?

The brain is linked to all parts of the body through the nervous system. If the mind is at ease this reflects itself on its physical mechanism, the brain, and is communicated through the brain to all parts of the body. Equally, of course, if the mind is not at ease this is also communicated through the brain to the body and causes disharmony, with resultant illness, in the body. Most physical illnesses are, in fact, psychosomatic and that is why spiritual healing can be effective in curing them.

Pain and suffering generally are only of value if they help souls to grow in awareness. I am all in favour of growth being achieved with as little pain as possible. My hope is that these sessions will help at least some people to raise their awareness to such a level that they will no longer need pain and suffering.

ELIMINATING OF THE SUBCONSCIOUS

2nd – 12th June: A conclusion to be drawn from the last session, I hope, is that healing is primarily a matter of raising awareness if it is to be effective in the long term. Obviously, then, the elimination of the subconscious (non-awareness) is the most important function of healing.

I have already recommended analysis of daily experiences in communication with guides as a means of reducing the extent of subconscious control. I would now like to suggest a development of that communication through the following steps: –

Ask your guides:
1. To tell you what are the areas of subconscious influence in so far as you are concerned. Just ask the question simply and wait for the answer. It will flow in unmistakably in the form of thoughts or impressions, or visual images;
2. To let you know the main area of influence;
3. To let you know how this area of influence originated. The answer may bring you face to face with painful memories, or create in you sensations of discomfort. Don't try to escape from these. Look at them and analyse them objectively and non-judgmentally until you no longer have anything to fear from them;
4. Whether that area of influence has been eliminated. If not, repeat the process. If it has, observe the effect for some time (a few weeks, at least) on the way you feel, then ask your guides to let you know the next biggest area of influence and go ahead and get rid of that in the same way.

The first and second steps are easy. Just write down what's given to you.

The third step is more difficult and may take some time to accomplish. I suggest that once you have put the question to your guides you should just wait and a way of answering your question will present itself. The answer may be given to you in a dream, or in a visual image while you're awake, or through an experience which would be a re-enactment of the experience from which the area of influence originated, or by direct communication from your guides, or by means of counselling. While the methods of providing answers may vary, you can be sure of one thing – they will be given. A person's guides will always find the best way to help him.

The fourth step is again easy.

In the last session I said that the higher the level of awareness the less pain and suffering there was. This may seem to conflict with what I said in an earlier session to the effect that at the level of full awareness the sharing of experience is maximised – for instance, that the suffering experienced by one soul still climbing the ladder of awareness is also experienced in a very real way by all souls at the top of the ladder, although not in the same way; an apt illustration may be what happens to parents whose child is suffering intense pain; the parents don't experience the child's pain, but their suffering is also intense. If every soul had regained full awareness there would be no pain and suffering. As the level of awareness is raised there will be less occasion for pain and suffering.

THE PHYSICAL BODY

16th – 18th June: One statement which is a matter of trust, but I hope also of reason, and two statements which don't have to depend on either trust or reason: a physical body is the agency which a soul uses for a lifetime on earth; all bodies have common characteristics and features; they are divided into two categories, male and female.

As has already been outlined, human beings were a product of the second stage of evolution. The pattern of male and female bodies and of physical reproduction had been set at the first stage. The second stage is, or course, a development of the first and the integrated soul needs a more sophisticated type of body than those provided at the first stage.

The body is a functional unit which operates according to an automatic pattern built into the overall grand design. The process of conception and birth, growth and decline happens as a matter of course which has come to be known as the natural order of things. Even when a body dies it is transformed into something else, dust or ashes, and is absorbed into the cycle of growth and rebirth. Nothing ever dies, in fact, only changes its form.

As the body is all that can usually be seen it is a logical enough proposition that the body is all there is. By now, however, I would hope that I have established, even from a purely rational point of view, that life is a continuity of which the death of the physical body is merely a stage or point of transition on the way.

The division of the human race into male and female was not done solely for reproductive purposes. More important, the grand designers felt that the adjustments which each of the sexes would have to make in living and sharing with and understanding each other, as well as caring for and coping with their families, would provide a wider variety of learning experiences than would be available for one sex on its own. The overall grand design was, of course, envisaged before the first stage was instituted and the male and female elements were built into it from the beginning.

The physical pleasure which human beings get from their bodies is also part of the design. People often allow themselves to get agitated over so-called unnatural practices between human beings, for instance, homosexuality. As with pain, pleasure is only experienced by the brain which is neither male or female. From a purely natural – as distinct from awareness – point of view, the stimulus which the brain uses as an immediate source of pleasure is of no consequence.

Practices such as contraception and deliberate abortion are regarded by many as interfering with natural laws and, particularly in the case of abortion, as murder. Obviously, these practices prevent births. Equally obviously, they don't interfere with the continuity of life since that is not dependent on physical happenings. No soul is in a position, or has a right, to make judgments about the practices or the people who perform them. Spiritually, the only importance which the practices have is their effect on individual awareness.

It is an inescapable fact that the physical body is subject to death. What is not generally realized is that, as a rule, souls not alone decide on whether they will incarnate or reincarnate in a physical body and the design of that body but also on the timing and manner of the body's death. In reality, therefore, the death of the body is self-determined.

When life is seen in the context of its spiritual continuity the significance of the body can be put into its proper perspective. It is clearly important as a vehicle by which the soul has chosen to further its spiritual development. On the other hand, the disintegration or death of the body is no tragedy – although, of course, the physical separation at death is a source of distress. Realisation of the purpose of physical life on earth and the relationship of the body to the soul should do much to lessen the distress.

REINCARNATION – III: TIME

2nd October. Two questions suggest themselves:

1) if everything is constantly happening now in an eternal present how can there be such a thing as reincarnation unless each soul is in some way fragmented into different personalities?;
2) if the concept of time does not exist in reality – that is, in spirit – why is it a part of the earth scene?

To take the second question first: earth was designed as a vehicle for learning experiences; a linear time sequence was a simple aid to learning; one experience would follow another and the lessons of each would be absorbed in an orderly way. Always the primary object is growth in awareness; the progression of time as you know it is simply a device to help to achieve that object.

Even on earth, however, there are clear reflections of a continuing present. Day repeats itself into night and season into season; the earth keeps on moving round the sun; thus an appearance of change is created so that it can truthfully be said in apparently contradictory terms that everything in nature changes but yet remains the same. If the earth were to stop moving, time would stand still; in other words, earth and time travel hand in hand.

Imagine earth as a merry-go-round. You jump on (are born) at one point and jump off (die) at another. You may jump on and off many times during the course of the round.

Now imagine that before you jump on each time you change your appearance in some way so that outwardly you seem to be a different person. At many stages during the round you appear in different guises.

Suppose that a spirit is looking down from above the merry-go-round. He sees you getting on and off in all your different appearances. He sees you creating an illusion of movement without actually going anywhere. He himself is neither taking up space nor moving through time. For him time and space have no meaning; for you the timing of your getting on and off and the space and appearance you choose each time on the merry-go-round are most significant.

However, if you see time and space in a different way - as a creative process of mental development and expansion - then the words have meaning within the reality of spirit. Each physical incarnation is intended as a process of development. In the wider meaning of time, therefore, physical existences of one soul cannot be said to take place simultaneously any more than they do in the physical time scale. The passage of time is really a record of progression towards the ultimate objective of full awareness. Physical existence illustrates the progression in a simple way with its framework of time and space, i.e., movement from one point to the next to the next, and so on in a linear sequence.

Spirit is endlessly creative; so that if you equate time with creativity rather than with movement from day to night, etc., then time is a fact of all life - physical and spirit - and there is no confusion of meaning.

When you are jumping on and off the merry-go-round you change your appearance each time. You shed the outer shell but you do not fragment the real you. As you grow in awareness, you also shed the attributes which had previously clouded your awareness; but they are no part of you nor were they ever although you may have hugged them to you for centuries (e.g., possessiveness, intolerance). As I explained in an earlier session, fragmentation of soul was a product of the original fall from awareness; given free will, it can still happen but it is not likely to because of the flexibility of the grand design in adjusting itself to the vagaries of free will. The fully aware soul is an integrated entity and will always remain so. Once a soul reaches the second stage it is also an integrated entity and it is unlikely that the grand design will fail to ensure that it remains so until it reaches full awareness.

One of the hallmarks of creativity is simplicity. Any concept of an entity endlessly fragmenting itself into different personalities is too complex to be creative in any positive sense of the word. I leave you to submit the matter to your own reasoning processes.

CHRISTIANITY

13th – 16th October. Christianity is founded on the belief that God sent his only son to become man and to be crucified, thereby taking on himself the sins of mankind and by his death and resurrection opening the gates of heaven to redeemed man. God is the Creator, a separate Being. Man is the created, made in the image of God but wholly inferior to Him.

During the 1900 odd years since its foundation Christianity has found expression in different religions but has retained its belief in the separation of God from man, of creator from creation.

In our sessions I have emphasised the oneness of God and man, the unity of creator and creation. A Christian reading the records of our sessions is faced with a dilemma; if his reason and/or his knowing tell him that my outline contains truth for him, his belief in orthodox Christianity must be shaken since, on the face of things, there seems to be no way in which the two positions can be reconciled.

Fundamentally, Christianity, as it has developed, does not reflect the teachings of Jesus Christ. However, as I have already pointed out, nothing happens by accident. It was a part of the grand design that Jesus should have come on earth and taught as he did; equally, it was a part of the grand design, *continually adjusting itself in line with the effects of free will,* that his teachings should have been interpreted as they have been since his time on earth.

Again I must repeat myself - life on earth is a learning experience.
The events of earth, the happenings, the teachings are in themselves or in isolation unimportant; they assume importance

because of the effects they create on the awareness of individual souls. Thus it is that, for instance, you can change your past not because you can change the events in your past but because you can change the effects they had on you.

By and large, people have not believed in themselves. They wanted to believe in a power outside of themselves which regulated birth and death and much of what happened in between. Orthodox Christianity met that need; if the need did not exist, Christianity would not have developed the way it did.

The sole object of the grand design is to help souls to raise their awareness levels to the stage where they will no longer need help. The design is infinitely flexible and responsive in the means by which it provides help. If you want to believe in an external force regulating your life then you will be helped within your pattern of belief. You will also be helped in your pattern of non-belief if you choose not to believe in anything beyond life on earth.

Jesus spoke much of his oneness with the Father. He also impressed on his listeners that they could be as he was. For later generations he became identified with the Father in oneness of Father and only Son whereas, of course, what he was teaching was the oneness, in common with him, of all souls with the Father. He became the redeemer, the interceder with the Father, the apparently human but really not human face of God; in order to preserve the idea of his separateness from humanity, the concept that God could not become an ordinary human being, his birth, death and resurrection were portrayed as miraculous events contrary to the natural order of things.

There is no doubt but that Christian beliefs as they have evolved have helped more souls to raise their levels of awareness (not least by providing a consciousness of continuing life) than if the teachings of Jesus had been interpreted as he intended them to be at the time he outlined them - otherwise the grand design would have found ways of correcting the misinterpretations. Is this not in some way making a mockery of Jesus? No; his level of awareness was such that he knew who and what he was. His purpose was to help others to reach his state. They did not believe in themselves as he believed in himself. Because of the certainty of his belief in himself, the aura of understanding which he conveyed, they exalted him since they felt that they could not be as he was. He was true to himself; therefore he could not be mocked or belittled in any real way. He fulfilled his purpose; it is unimportant that it was fulfilled in ways which he did not himself envisage during his life on earth.

In spite of what might be taken as appearances to the contrary souls are progressing through the various stages of development at an increasingly faster rate. Much of the apparent chaos and turbulence of modern life is a reflection of the inadequacy of traditional beliefs as they are now perceived. Those beliefs still play their part and will continue to do so but on an ever-decreasing scale. It is like the storm before the calm rather than the other way round. More and more souls are searching for beliefs with deeper meaning for themselves. Ultimately their search will only end when they accept with an inner realisation that knows no contradiction that they are one with all life and with the source of all life.

Total acceptance of oneness rather than separation is the key which opens the door to progression beyond a certain level of awareness.

SECOND COMING?

20th – 24th October. From the beginning of Christianity what has been popularly called the Second Coming has been mooted. It has been variously associated with a Final Judgment Day and with renewals of spirituality. One way or another it has been generally believed by those who adhere to Christianity that Jesus will come again to earth in some form.

Of course, there will be no Judgment Day, final or otherwise.

Ultimately, however, there will be a time of great rejoicing when all souls will have regained full awareness. This will be wholeness of individuality as part of the wholeness of wholeness. I make no predictions as to when that time will come; in one sense it is already here, given the grand design; in another, it is a long way off, given free will.

What gave rise to the belief in a second coming was the fact that while Jesus ostensibly came to save the world it was obviously not saved by the time he left it. On one level, then, it was an apparently logical thing that he should have left his teachings after him, given souls a chance to receive and follow them and eventually sit in judgment on them, taking those who faithfully followed his teachings with him to eternal happiness in heaven and condemning those who failed to do so to eternal damnation in hell. On another level, it was also logical that he would wish to come again to finish what he had started, to implement such a massive spiritual renewal that all would be saved the next time round.

It is a downgrading of the nature of any individual soul to believe that it can be saved (to use the common terminology) by any act or series of actions of another, no matter how meritorious. *There is no*

39

escaping from the fact that each soul has to find its own salvation – in other words, its own wholeness of awareness. It can be, and is, helped, of course, but no amount of help is of any use to it unless it receives it and reacts to it in a positive way.

I don't exclude the possibility that Jesus will at some stage decide on another earthly experience, not as a saviour but in order to help others to help themselves. I can tell you that it is not at present envisaged by the grand design that he should do so and I think it is most unlikely that he will since he has now progressed beyond the fourth stage.

In a totally spiritual sense, however, the concept of a second coming is very real. It is a continuum in that he is, of course, ceaselessly helping others. He has gone past the stage where it would be possible for him to pass judgment on any soul. Judgment is a feature of non-awareness.

GRACE

26th – 30th October. Being in a state of grace is commonly equated with being free from sin. Grace is regarded as a gift from God, most powerfully conferred by sacraments - for example, the sacrament of baptism is said to free a child from original sin and thereby make it possible for it to get to Heaven. (I should have said a person rather than a child, but people normally think of baptism in connection with children.)

The rite of baptism is symbolic. Think of sin as separation from self (or God). Original sin, then, was what gave rise to the initial separation, that is, the fall from awareness as described in an earlier session. Water is the material expression of spirituality. The pouring of water over the child signifies the spiritual nature of the child. It also signifies the cleansing of the child from what separates it from its true (spiritual) nature.

In ultimate terms, baptism is a ritualistic dramatisation of what is inevitable, the regaining of full awareness or the attainment of heaven, whichever way you like to look at it.

Unfortunately, however, baptism (or any sacrament) is only symbolic and does not – cannot – have the miraculous power attributed to it. I say unfortunately because it would be a very easy shortcut if it had; but that would, of course, be an interference with the freedom of the individual soul. The existence of free will means that each soul makes its own choices, even if they lead to hell rather than heaven in terms of non-awareness as opposed to awareness.

Incidentally, do you think that people really believe in the power of baptism? If they do, why don't they wish that their children should die in infancy and thus be spared the risk of Hell? And where does Infinite Justice fit into a situation where an infant who dies without having had an opportunity to commit sin may go straight to Heaven through the power of baptism and a person who survives to adulthood is faced with all sorts of occasions of sin and by succumbing to even one of them may go to Hell for all eternity?

Yet religious rites, sacraments, etc., serve a purpose. They are signposts to the eternal nature of life. They point the soul towards a realisation of its higher potential. They are a source of help to souls to shed burdens of guilt and worry and despair and loneliness. I don't mean to be frivolous when I say that they have been, and are, to many adults what Santa Claus is to many children - a reaching out of the imagination beyond all the bounds of rationality and an opening of the mind to things beyond the day-to-day routine of existence.

Even as it takes part in all the rituals, however, and no matter how wholehearted it is in the observance of them, the mind has an inner knowing that it is suspending a part of itself. For some time it will manage to still half-formed questionings with the much resorted to answer that what cannot be explained is a mystery, with another part of the circle of non-answers being that a mystery is what cannot be explained. Eventually, however, the mind will not be satisfied with evasions - and then it is really on the road to increased awareness. Anything that stimulates the mind to ask questions is helpful; thus also are the rituals a source of help, albeit an unconsciously indirect one.

I would define a state of grace as a feeling of oneness with all life, a harmonious condition in which all beings, things, happenings have their own place and are allowed to unfold themselves without interference. It is not a passive condition; rather it is active in the most effective possible way in that it is flowing with life, the creativity of life, and not a frustrating misuse of energy in attempting to swim against the tide.

An illustration may be helpful. Unknown to each other two men are travelling by train on the same journey. As all the seats are occupied they have to stand. Each of them has a rather heavy case with him. One man holds the case, changing it from hand to hand, for the duration of the journey, about an hour. He endures the journey impatiently and when he reaches his destination he is tired, his hands are sore, his case feels heavier than ever and he is generally in bad humour. The second man leaves his case on the floor and decides to enjoy the journey to the best of his ability. When his trip is over his case feels light and he is good-humoured and relaxed.

This little story can be looked at in different ways.

For example, the journey symbolises a lifetime on earth. Both men are born at the same time and die at the same time. The train is the spiritual help available to them all through life. The cases are the subconscious elements of their minds.

The first man makes no use of the train (his spiritual help) in order to relieve him of the burden of his case (subconscious). By the time he reaches the end of the journey (dies) his case is heavier and he is in worse condition than he was when he decided to start the journey (reincarnate).

The second man, however, uses the train to relieve him of the burden of his case. At the end of the journey the case is lighter and he is happier.

On another level, the train symbolises the harmonious pattern of movement and change in all life. The first man endures it impatiently and gets no benefit from it. The second man flows with it and gets considerable benefit from it.

The second man is more likely to be in a state of grace, as I have defined it, than the first man.

FREE WILL IN THE GRAND DESIGN

1st – 6th November: In earlier sessions I have talked about free will and what a key element it is in the nature of soul. I also said that nothing happened by accident. Even though we have gone into this before I can see that there is still some confusion in your mind about a possible contradiction between those two statements.

Forgive me if I go back a little over ground already covered. Once a soul evolves into the second stage its free will is again operative. This means that it has freedom of choice in all circumstances. For example, it chooses to reincarnate. Before doing so it plans, with the help of guides if it so wishes, the course of its life on earth and it agrees with its guides – if it has chosen to have guides – that they will help it to follow that course. On earth it has forgotten – at least on the surface – both the plan and the guides, but it still has free will.

Let's suppose that as part of its plan a soul has chosen to become a priest and take a vow of celibacy for the primary purpose of overcoming an obsession with sex. (Here I must remind you that all obsessions are of the mind and therefore carried through into spirit if they are not overcome during a lifetime on earth.) During his early life on earth his environmental conditions as well as his own inner knowledge of his plan and the efforts of his guides steer him in the direction of the priesthood. Yet his obsession is still there and eventually he chooses to renounce the idea of becoming a priest. By an act of free will he has now reached a position where he has deviated from his life plan.

The important thing to remember, however, is that becoming a priest was only the means by which he had hoped to overcome his obsession. Now the flexibility of the grand design and its immediate agents, his guides, comes into operation. The guides continually engineer situations which will serve as learning experiences for him. They never lose sight of his main purpose on earth which is to free himself from his obsession even though he himself may continue to indulge the obsession by his own acts of free will.

But suppose he marries and has children; in view of the fact that his plan was to become a priest there was surely no agreement made in spirit with other souls about marriage and children? In a case like this it is likely that the girl who agrees to marry him is also acting contrary to her life plan; and that the children who are born to them will have decided to avail themselves of an unscheduled opportunity to reincarnate rather than wait for the usual arrangements to be made for them. Even given the rather non-ideal circumstances of their reincarnation, however, the children will also have decided on their own life plan – with, of course, the help of guides if so desired.

Generally speaking, people get married and children are born to them in accordance with arrangements made in spirit. The exceptions are rare. Obviously many marriages are unstable even from a very early stage. Nonetheless, it is likely that they are the fulfilment of pre-arranged plans. Divorces and re marriages are also likely to have been planned in advance. They are all learning experiences.

Marriage and children are obviously central issues in the lives of many people on earth. Work is another. As a general rule, each soul, prior to reincarnation, chooses, with the help of its guides, the pattern of its entire working life on earth. One of the functions of the guides is to help the soul – now in a physical body – to follow that pattern. Because of free will there are deviations from the pattern in many cases; but, by and large, these are only minor deviations and it is true as a generalisation to say that each and every soul on earth is in the best place and in the best work (or non-work) environment for it to fulfil its life purpose. It is, broadly speaking, relatively easy for guides to arrange what I might categorise as environmental or situational conditions such as work or marriage. The real difficulty is in helping souls to help themselves to benefit from the experiences which they themselves have chosen.

I must emphasise that in making their arrangements the guides are not in any way controlling or seeking to control a person's will. They are merely helping him to live his life under the conditions chosen by him prior to his birth. If, during his life on earth, a person's choice of action conflicts with his plan his guides will not seek to influence his decision but will instead seek to put opportunities in his way which will help him to achieve his life purpose even if he chooses to deviate from his plan.

I would like to make two points in support of my statement that nothing happens by accident - or, perhaps put more clearly, that nothing that happens is an accident. First, every action involves an expression of choice, of free will. Second, even if an action is in conflict with a chosen plan it still serves as a means of furthering a soul's life purpose due to the flexibility of the grand design in using each action, no matter how negative it may seem to be, as the basis of an opportunity to raise awareness.

The word accident is most commonly used in today's world in connection with car crashes. Suppose a man leaves his home and drives with the utmost care on his usual route to work. He leaves his home at exactly the same time each morning, travels at the same speed and on the same route. He follows this pattern without incident for many years. Then one morning another car crashes into his. He is entirely blameless in so far as the crash is concerned; nevertheless he is severely injured.

How can my statement that nothing happens by accident be reconciled with that incident?

The man was in his car on the road by his own choice, an act of free will on his part. This was as true on the morning of the crash as it was on every other morning. It was entirely his own choice that he should follow a particular pattern of operation consistently each morning. It may well have been part of his plan that he should have been involved in the crash – for instance, as a means of compelling him to question his values and attitudes. In any event, whether it was or it wasn't part of his plan, his guides will use it to help him achieve the purpose for which he reincarnated.

It is obviously much easier for human beings if they can stay with their plans. That's why I keep on stressing the importance of tuning in to guidance and as far a possible living in a state of grace or oneness with all life.

PROPHECY – I

10th – 14th November. Trying to foretell the future is as old as time; that's an appropriate way of putting it since it's only in a framework of time that prophecy comes into its own.

Through the ages many seers and prophets have made many predictions, some accurate, some partly so, and some completely off the mark. In particular, there are various predictions about the last part of the present century which would seem to presage dire happenings, followed in some predictions by the end of the world and Judgment Day, and in others by a New Age, perhaps a Golden Age.

Of course, in human terms every day there are dire happenings as there have been since life on earth began. But the predictions generally foretell more cataclysmic events far beyond what is already happening.

How does prophecy occur? One common ground that prophets seem to have is that their prophecies come to them or through them from a higher source. Now let's go back briefly to the visualisation of life on earth as a merry-go-round with a soul in spirit looking down on it. It sees what's happening at each stage of the round. For instance, in the case of a person getting on at a particular point the soul looking down can see the pattern of events which are likely to unfold for that person while he stays on the round; as it can also see what's happening at all stages on the round it can see the past and future progression of the person on the round; what seems to be a prophecy to the person who is, say, at point X is really only a description of what's happening at point Y from the viewpoint of the soul looking down.

That's prophecy reduced to very simple terms in order to give you an understanding of how it works. There is nothing psychic or mystifying about it - think of the merry-go-round.

Generally speaking, all prophecy can do is outline a likely pattern of events. If people are working with their plans, then it is relatively easy to see how they will fit into the pattern; even if they are not, it is still possible to predict how they will react to a given situation in line with the way they normally express themselves through their free will.

If you visualise life on earth as a merry-go-round then you can see that what you call the past must also be the future. For instance, if you get on at point A and go on to points B, C, etc., when you reach point C point B will be in your past. However, at some stage you may again get on at point A; then point B will be in your future. Thus do events and civilisations keep on repeating themselves. Souls change, their reaction to events change and they progress in awareness through the experiencing of events which appear to be changing but are really repeating themselves - as in the natural order of things (seasons, grass, flowers, etc.).

Is all that clear enough? I hope you can see now why prophecy is no big deal. In the final analysis it can be reduced to two factors - (1) astuteness of interpretation on the part of souls in spirit in the reading of patterns of behaviour and fitting them into events, and (2) clarity of communication between these souls and persons on earth. In the second factor I include the capacity of persons on earth to receive and interpret accurately what they receive.

Well, then, are all these catastrophes going to happen, as foretold, before the end of the present century? What does your reason tell you?

The acceleration of growth in technology in the present century has increased the possibilities or more devastating conflicts. Such conflicts have happened, are happening, and will continue to happen. However, there will be no cataclysmic happening, such as the end of the world, in this century - nor, indeed, in any century. Ultimately, of course, life on earth as you know it will cease but that will not happen until it no longer serves as a learning experience, and then it will be a gradual process of evolution, a natural process.

As I have said in an earlier session, the process of growth in awareness has also accelerated and will continue to do so. Revolutions in thinking are already taking place and in this sense it can be said that earth is moving into a golden age. But there will be no such thing as separating the goats from the sheep; one of the big advantages of life on earth for growth purposes is that souls at different levels of awareness come into contact with each other with beneficial effects for those at the lower levels; it would be unthinkable that the grand design would exclude any soul, or group of souls, from the possibility of continuing benefit.

PROPHECY – II

29th November – 5th December: In the last session I outlined how prophecy happens. Why is there so much hit and miss about it? Surely it is possible for a soul looking down on the merry-go-round to foresee that certain events will happen even allowing for the free will of the people involved since within the context of a continuing present these events are already happening? For instance, is the soul not able to see newspaper headlines as they will be?

The most important thing to be said is that it is not possible for any soul, no matter what its level of awareness, to predict with a 100% degree of accuracy what's going to happen and when it's going to happen. This is, of course, because of free will. For instance, the only thing I can predict with certainty is that all souls must eventually get back to full awareness; I make that prediction because it is not possible that souls can exist indefinitely in a condition contrary to their nature and also because the grand design is so comprehensive and flexible and its pattern of success is so well established that I cannot envisage failure for it even in respect of one soul. But I have no idea as to when my prediction will be fulfilled - except that there is a long time to go yet.

Suppose that I'm a soul looking down on the merry-go-round. I can see events as they are happening to people at a certain stage on the round and I can see that they are likely to repeat themselves for people coming up to that stage. But because people may not continue to behave in accordance with their previous patterns some of the events may not happen to them at all or they may happen in a different way or according to a different time scale; so my prediction may be totally wrong or I may get it right in some respects or I may get it right except for the timing. I cannot foresee newspaper headlines since I'm not in the habit of influencing newspaper editors or sub-editors as to what to put into the headlines!

A person's guides are much better able to predict that person's future than they are able to predict happenings, e.g., on a global scale, which are not directly connected with the person. The reason for this is that the person will have drawn up his life plan in conjunction with his guides. To the extent that he is staying with his plan his future is easier or harder to predict. (Incidentally, the sense of destiny which many people feel is accounted for by their inner knowledge of their plan - their plan is their destiny.)

As I have said on previous occasions guides will never impose their will on another soul even if that soul is deviating from his plan. This is not true of souls at lower levels of awareness. Thus, a person may get a message from a spirit source that such and such is going to happen to him. He is then mentally conditioned to the event and the soul in spirit in its state of unawareness will do all in its power to make it happen. The two influences working together will in all probability succeed and in this way a prediction is fulfilled.

Nothing happens without purpose since everything that happens is given a purpose within the overall flexibility of the grand design. Life is a wonderfully evolving thing, not subject to the rigidity of pre-ordination. The only element of pre-ordination is each soul's life plan and even that, as we have seen, can work within an unlimited framework of flexibility.

Of course, guides don't object to being questioned about the future. However, if the questioner shows a tendency towards being influenced in an obsessive way by the answers the guides will more than likely give him increasingly contradictory answers in order to help him to rid himself of his obsessions. Trying to live in the future does nothing to help a person fulfil his purpose on earth.

Souls in spirit are often not any wiser or more advanced than souls temporarily on earth but they are in a better position to see the overall picture of happenings on earth and therefore to make more accurate predictions about the future. The more aware a soul is the less likely it is to make predictions if there is any risk that they may influence the exercise of free will; however, if that risk is not present it will probably enjoy chancing its arm - or going out on a limb, if you prefer to put it that way!

MEMORY – II

20th December: I defined memory as the mind's way of remembering things. I also said that it acted as a screen between the conscious and the subconscious and that it would no longer be needed once the subconscious was eliminated altogether. It is obviously rather difficult for you to conceive of a situation in which memory doesn't operate but I'll try to explain what it's like.

With the elimination of the subconscious the soul is no longer prey to negativity, such as fear, resentment, anxiety, worry, guilt, hatred. Its consciousness, or awareness of itself, and of its place in God, is complete. This doesn't mean that a fundamental or magical change takes place; all it means is that the remaining veils of unawareness are lifted and the soul is once more conscious of being fully and completely itself and at one with all souls and all life. The soul doesn't miraculously know everything. It does, however, have access to all knowledge since all knowledge is contained within the collective consciousness of all souls and the aware soul knows where to find the answer to what it wants to know at any given time.

In your terms I know who I am which includes knowing what I have been and what I will be. I am a spirit being of feeling from which follows thought. My thoughts which emanate from me - which are myself as an expression of me – lead me towards certain directions of interest; anything I want to explore along those lines of interest I can do by tapping into the collective consciousness. Thus I evolve. When I move from one line of interest to another I retain my knowledge of the first line although I may exclude it from my consciousness if I wish while I'm concentrating on the second line. I don't have any memory obstacle to overcome.

A parallel with your situation would go rather like this. Suppose that yesterday you researched a certain project. Today every detail is still vivid in your mind even though you are working on something different. While you are working you exclude yesterday's project completely from your consciousness but, if you wish to do so, you can comprehensively recall all the details of it. Memory has not yet created a barrier to recall. To me all is as yesterday – or, more accurately, today. That is, in fact, total consciousness. Memory – or forgetfulness if you like – is no longer necessary.

MIRACLES

31st December, 1982 – 3rd January, 1983: It is, I suppose, rather obvious from our previous sessions what my line on miracles is. Nonetheless, it might be helpful to devote a little time and space (in a manner of speaking) to the subject.

Miracles are usually understood to be extraordinary happenings beyond the natural order of things; for example, the healing of a person who, according to all known medical tests, was incurably ill. Generally, the reversal of a physical trend or the changing of a physical substance from one form to another is involved; dramatic examples are the raising of Lazarus from the dead and the changing of water into wine at the wedding feast of Cana.

Miracles are often associated with places of pilgrimage. Again the emphasis is on physical healing.

Because most illnesses are psychosomatic, dramatic changes, sometimes classified as miracles, take place regularly in physical organisms. The mind controls the fate of the body. If the mind decides that the body is going to be sick, it will be sick; If the mind decides that the body is going to be well, it will be well unless, of course, it is part of its life plan that it should endure a particular physical deficiency as a learning experience.

You say that nobody can really want to be sick; yet you know that that isn't so. How many people use sickness as a means of opting out of situations with which they feel they can't cope? Or as a means of winning sympathy or attention for themselves? Or as a response to a subconscious influence, such as fear?

I will make a very general statement which you may find hard to accept; if healing doesn't happen in the mind it will not happen in the body. It is unlikely that anybody who is ill will admit – least of all to himself – that he doesn't want to be well, that his illness has become a crutch or an obsession with him. So until he finds a meaning in life which will enable him to release himself from the obsession and to convince himself that he doesn't need the crutch anymore his mind will not be healed and therefore his body will not be healed. Healers or places of pilgrimage may help the mind to free itself with beneficial results for the body.

Take, for example, the case of a woman who is suffering from arthritis and who joins in a pilgrimage to Lourdes. She doesn't profess to believe in any existence beyond that of earth and only goes on the pilgrimage out of curiosity, with no faith in any possibility of cure for herself or for others. She takes part in all the rituals and, to her surprise, she finds herself cured of her arthritis. How can this be explained in the light of what I have already said?

The physical facts of the case are simply stated. Before the pilgrimage, the woman suffered severe pain and physical restriction from arthritis. After the pilgrimage she had no pain and could move her limbs freely.

The most likely explanation is as follows. The woman had chosen as part of her life plan to acquire arthritis and to let herself be healed of it in this way so that she could bear witness to it. Her witness would be all the more effective because of her previously-known scepticism. The healing was carried out by her guides and perhaps other spirit helpers. She had already accepted it and willed that it should happen to her.

The whole physical scene was born out of the grand design. As a general rule, there is no interference with what has come to be known as the natural order of things. However, as I keep saying, the design is infinitely flexible and if those souls who are coordinating its implementation consider that an odd miracle will help the progress of the design then so it happens through specially-selected channels, part of whose plan on earth this will have been. Obviously, if miracles are to have any effect they can't happen too often or they will be as readily accepted and overlooked as the wonders of nature. Really miraculous events such as the birth of a child or the blooming of a rose have been taken for granted because they are commonplace. But if these things can happen, is it any wonder that other things which are marvelled at because of their rarity can also happen? The working of what are deemed miracles is not difficult for spirit. How could it be since all matter is a creation of spirit?

GOD – III

4th January; Today you are concerned because there seems to be a conflict between what I have told you about God – my definition of God – and what you have read in a book apparently emanating from a spirit source. The book outlines various hierarchical structures within the realms of spirit with One Supreme Being demanding worship as the Lord and Source and Creator of all. In my definition there is no hierarchy; all souls are equal and are a manifestation of God, or love, or feeling and all its expressions; there is no Supreme Being; temporarily, the Father (or the 99% of all souls who never lost awareness or who have fully regained it) is the source of help for the 1% who have yet to regain full awareness.

You are primarily concerned in case you may be the cause of misleading others who may happen to read the records of our sessions.

There is no doubt but that what you have read is closer to the teachings of orthodox religions than my definition.

The world of spirit is vast and varied. Many souls on the journey back to full awareness are at different levels of awareness. Those at higher levels are helping those below them on the ladder; help is flowing all the way down from the Father. There is a coordination of effort within the grand design. Some souls have agreed to act as coordinators. For this reason they may seem to be ranked higher than others and since the coordinators at one level are themselves being coordinated at another level and so on you can see how there could appear to be a hierarchical spirit structure.

There is also the fact that the higher a soul's level of awareness the more this is reflected in the aura of radiance it manifests. A soul at, say, the second stage coming into contact with a soul at the fourth stage will readily assume that that soul is a higher being than itself. The road to self-acceptance is a long and difficult one for most souls and involves finding comprehensive and satisfying answers to such questions as - who am I? how did I come to exist? what is my place in the whole scheme of things? what is my relationship to others? There is no place for false pride or false humility in self-acceptance.

I understand and sympathise with your concern – which is also mine – that you should not mislead others. I could try to reassure you by saying that since you are acting as a channel for me the responsibility is mine - but, of course, you are well aware that you share the responsibility by agreeing to put my thoughts into words and to record them. And you can't even see me so that you have neither the consolation of visual proof of my existence nor the possibility of forming a judgment about my integrity by face-to-face contact!

Since the other spirit source and I – and indeed most sources – agree that the answers to all questions lie within why not put that to the test and meditate on questions such as those I posed above? If you do that and if you continue with these sessions it will presumably mean that the answers you got were in line with what I have told you.

POSSESSION

11th – 15th January: Demon possession and exorcism have been consistently matters of fascination for many people through the centuries. The belief is that a spirit, usually regarded as evil, takes possession of a human being and influences his behaviour, and that the spirit may be forced to leave by a ritualistic practice known as exorcism.

You may remember that in one of our earliest sessions I said that the only demons in existence were creatures of the subconscious. So the first point I will make is that it is not possible for anybody to be possessed by a devil since there is no such being as a devil or evil spirit.

There are, of course, souls at low levels of awareness who act mischievously and often maliciously towards others. This is as true of the spirit world as it is of earth. Souls in spirit try to influence souls temporarily living as human beings on earth as indeed do human beings try to influence souls in spirit (notably by prayer). There is constant interaction between souls irrespective of whether they are in spirit or on earth. The only difference is that the influence being used by a spirit source is usually not obvious to human beings.

All forms of influence - in the sense of imposition or attempted imposition of one will on another or others - are expressions of non-awareness (or evil, if you want to be dramatic about it).

What is called possession is usually agitation of the subconscious although it is, of course, possible for a spirit entity to control the mind of a human being, if it is allowed to do so. However, it cannot take possession of the body, nor can it even share it with the soul whose preserve it is even if that soul invites it to do so. The design of the body is such that only one soul (mind) can inhabit it, and if that soul decided to leave the body in order to allow another to possess it the body would die. So possession in the sense of physical possession as it is commonly understood is a myth.

My second point then is that whatever exorcism does, or claims to do, it does not drive any alien spirit, evil or otherwise, out of a body.

There are many instances of human beings hearing voices which seem to give expression to malicious thoughts and convey urgings to murder or suicide or other apparently sinister forms of behaviour. The voices are not really voices in the physical sense; probably a more accurate description of them would be thought-forms. They are likely to be projections from the subconscious and/or communications from spirit sources. If the subconscious gains control it may run riot as it often does in dreams; if the control extends into the waking hours, imbalance, which in an extreme form is insanity, occurs. The person who is in a state of imbalance is often an easy prey for an unaware spirit which may well succeed in imposing its will on him and will probably be most reluctant to stop doing so.

A feature of exorcism as practised is that it usually tends to be a lengthy process. It sometimes achieves success for that very reason, because the invading spirit sees no future in staying around and having to endure repeated rituals directed at it. In effect, what happens is that the spirit is persecuting its human victim and now, in turn, it is being persecuted - which, of course, doesn't appeal to it at all!

To some it seems a tidy arrangement that souls in spirit should be in one place and human beings in another, but that's not the way things are. Spirit beings at different levels of awareness are constantly around human beings although they are mostly about their own business and have no interest in, or indeed no consciousness of, what human beings are doing. Some spirit beings, however, remain obsessed with life on earth for years and they are likely to attach themselves to anybody who will entertain them, in a manner of speaking. Human beings are influenced by such spirits; sometimes the spirits are acting in what they regard as the best interests of the humans, while other times, of course, they are simply acting mischievously or maliciously.

The traditional polarisation of good and evil has coloured people's thinking and created an attitude of hostility towards earthbound souls. In reality, of course, they are very much in need of help, and they are, in fact, often helped through their continued contact with human beings.

To anybody who accepts that he has guides I would strongly recommend that he ask them, if he has not already done so, not to allow any earthbound soul to invade his thoughts. Remember that the guides cannot interfere unless they are asked to do so. At the same time he can, if he so wishes, ask his guides to help him to use every opportunity to help any earthbound souls who might come to him, irrespective of whether they come for positive or negative reasons. It will be a team effort, of course – the guides will themselves also help the earthbound souls in so far as they allow themselves to be helped. In my view, this is the best any human being can do for his fellow souls in spirit.

What I want to emphasise most in this session is that all earthbound or unaware souls need to be treasured and loved rather than banished. If you reject any soul - again, to be dramatic, if you cast it into outer darkness - you are not being true to yourself (love) and are, in fact, separating yourself from life. Bear in mind, however, that you can only offer love - or, I should say, be love, which means having total respect for the free will of each and every soul with whom you come into contact.

COMMUNICATION WITH GUIDES

19th – 23rd January: In this session we might, perhaps, with advantage take a little time off from deeper metaphysical or philosophical questions and dwell briefly on how to improve communication with guidance.

I realise that throughout our sessions I have possibly laboured the point about the desirability of regular communication. I make no apology for doing so since I think it is the best way to increase awareness. Because I am such an earnest advocate of communication I feel that I should do everything in my power to show how the best possible communication can be achieved. There will be little new in the session – it is simply a matter of bringing together what is scattered through earlier sessions.

The first requirement is relaxation. If you're in a state of anxiety communication (of any kind) is difficult.

How to relax? Stand, or preferably sit, still. Take a few deep breaths, inhaling and exhaling gently. Let you mind go blank. Or imagine yourself in your favourite place doing what you like best to do - which may be nothing. Or count up to, say, a hundred. Or think of a very restful experience which you will probably have had at some time. Or listen to music, if that appeals to you. Or look at television, if you find that restful. Or read for a little while. Or take a walk. It's a matter of deciding what you find most restful and using that.

The next step depends on what form you wish the communication to take. If, for example, you would like to have some casual conversation with your guides you can do that simply by expressing your communications in thoughts and waiting for the answers which you will receive in thought form.

If, on the other hand, you have a specific problem on which you would like the advice of your guides, it is desirable that you should first define the problem clearly. It is good for your awareness to try to define your own problems – I prefer to call them challenges or, better still, learning experiences – yourself. However, if you are not clear as to what the problem is or if you find difficulty in defining it, I suggest that you ask your guides to do it for you and to give you their advice on it also.

If you have already adopted the suggestion I recommended in our last session about asking your guides not to let other spirit entities invade your thoughts except by arrangement, then there's no more to be done.

To summarise, the steps are:
i. ask your guides, if you have not already done so, not to let any other spirit entities invade your thoughts except by arrangement with you;
ii. relax, using whatever procedure best suits you;
iii. communicate by way of transmitting and receiving thoughts; and
iv. if you have a specific problem (learning experience) on which you need advice, try to define the problem first; if you are not able to do that, ask your guides to do it for you and to give you their advice on it.

If you follow these steps, you will find that with practice you will have no communication difficulties within a short period of time. I stress the words – with practice – because, as with every activity, there is no substitute for experience.

In conclusion, I would like to remind you that imagination is the language of the soul in case you might be inclined to dismiss valuable insights coming to you from your guides as being "just your imagination"!

THE FIRST STAGE: ELABORATION

27th – 30th January: In our sessions on the seven stages of awareness as I categorised them I passed over the first stage fairly briefly; some elaboration might be useful.

The first stage stretches from virtual non-awareness to a 50-50 state. This is the stage in which the soul is still fragmented, the non-human stage.

Because free will is not operative at the first stage all activities follow the original pattern laid down in the grand design. Many souls at different levels of awareness have taken on specific responsibilities in connection with the implementation of the grand design.

You may wish to refer back to the sessions on the creation of the world and on the stages of awareness in order to refresh yourself on how fragmentation occurred and how the way back to awareness is being orchestrated by the grand design.

Within the various forms of non-human life there are gradations of awareness and souls progress through the different forms in a most comprehensively-planned way until they reach a state where they are ready to integrate as individual souls and incarnate as human beings if they so wish. There is no element of chance in the non-human condition; things happen according to plan. Human beings interfere with the plan from time to time, especially by acts of cruelty, but adjustments are made to compensate for such interference.

A soul which has virtually lost all awareness is likely to incarnate in a multiplicity of physical bodies with short life expectancies. During its physical manifestations it will have made enough progress (mainly through the development of its instinct – e.g., for survival, for comfort, for food) – to be ready to incarnate in another species.

All the different species of non-human life were specially designed as vehicles for increasing awareness and are classified in order of ascending level. The needs of each soul were thoroughly explored and a plan was drawn up for it. The progress of each soul is monitored on an individual basis. It is no exaggeration to say that nothing happens - even the most apparently infinitesimal thing - which is not comprehended by the grand design either in its original planning or by adjustment. Once a species has served its purpose it becomes extinct.

The most numerous forms of physical life are found in the insect world. The least aware souls progress through perhaps several species of insects. Fish, bird and animal life intermingle in the classifications. The highest levels of awareness are reached, as you would expect, at the stage of domestic animals, such as dogs and cats. At that stage a soul has developed from multiple fragmentation to, usually, five or less; in other words, a soul may manifest itself temporarily in the physical bodies of, say, five dogs or cats - sometimes maybe only two. If there is enough love shown to them in their homes, they are likely to grow sufficiently in awareness to become reintegrated as one soul.

Many people will find it hard to accept that as souls (spiritual beings) they may have progressed through physical life forms which they find, at worst, repulsive and, at best, lovable but mindless. I would suggest to such people that they ask themselves what purpose do they see behind all the different species of life and how has it come about that there is such order and harmony in their world.

From an awareness point of view it is very important that the place of non-human life within all life should be recognised and accepted. It is also very important that each individual animal, bird, etc., should be treated with respect and love. It is just as important that humans should respect and love non-humans as that they should respect and love each other.

INTELLIGENCE: THE OVERSOUL – I

7th – 12th February: What is intelligence? The measure of capacity for receiving and retaining information? Mental alertness?

I would define intelligence as that quality which enables a person to receive, understand and communicate information. That I have included the communication of information may be somewhat surprising, but I think that it is a necessary ingredient; for example, it is not enough for a person undergoing a test or an examination to know the answers - he must be able to transfer his knowledge to the examiner in a readily understandable way.

Obviously, intelligence is a mental attribute. In earlier sessions I have said that the mind and soul were one and the same, that the brain was the physical mechanism used by the mind during an earth life and that the brain died with the body. Intelligence is linked with the brain and, accordingly, is only operative during earth existence.

The brain chosen by the mind (soul) for a particular earth life is specially designed for its life purpose. The fact that one person is more or less intelligent than another is no indication of levels of awareness.

So we have a mind (soul) which chooses a particular type of physical body to fulfil a planned life purpose, the body incorporates a brain and the brain manifests itself through intelligence.

When the body dies the mind (soul) is free of the body and free of the brain and the intelligence associated with the body. Does this mean that its (mental) condition may be completely changed? An example may help to clarify things.

Take a soul which in a particular life on earth achieved fame as a philosopher and a writer. His writings were particularly notable for the clarity of his thought. All who knew him or of him acknowledged the superiority of his intelligence and his mental capacity generally.

In the course of time he leaves his physical body and returns to his former spirit state. He evaluates his present state of awareness and the contribution which his most recent experience on earth has made to it. He finds that he has made some progress but that he has not succeeded in fulfilling his life purpose in that he has accepted other people's evaluation of him as a superior being. In order to counterbalance this he decides that he will reincarnate in a physical body with limited intelligence in an environment which encourages respect for those with high intelligence levels. So here we have the apparently incongruous situation of a man who was renowned for his intelligence in one lifetime being disregarded and downgraded because of his lack of intelligence in a later lifetime.

Once again he lives his life-span and passes on. It takes him some time to adjust to his changed condition. He responds well to the help available to him from his guides and other souls. Soon he throws off the shackles of his most recent earth condition and he is able to resume his former (mental) state with the added dimension accruing to it from his experience on earth.

A useful analogy in the physical sense is that of a person who becomes blind during an earth life. He is now operating with less than the capacity formerly available to him. Each and every soul which chooses to incarnate or reincarnate in a physical body is operating under restrictive conditions from which it will be freed on leaving the physical body. It will only retain the self-imposed mental restrictions.

The soul which presents itself to the world in a physical body only manifests itself to the extent that it has chosen to be restricted while it is on earth. In its earth manifestation it is really only revealing an aspect of itself with the other aspects in the background, although supportively so, while that one is being developed. When it returns to its spirit state it gradually reassumes all its aspects.

This is a rather difficult concept and I don't want to create any misunderstanding about it. There is no question of the soul being fragmented and a part of it being housed in a physical human body. It is just that, for instance, one particular quality is being developed and exclusively concentrated upon during a lifetime. If you think of an earth lifetime as a training course you will be able to grasp the idea more easily. Say you attend a course dealing with a particular subject such as interviewing skills. During the course you are concentrating exclusively on the development of those skills. At the same time all your other skills and all that constitutes your being are still there and are, in fact, supporting you during the course; only while you are concentrating on the course you are not conscious of your greater, more comprehensive, self.

The soul on earth is rather like a many-sided structure which is only showing one side of itself at a time. It remains the same soul when it resumes its non-physical condition but now it rediscovers its other sides. Accordingly, life in spirit is much more broadly based than on earth. While there are, of course, still different levels of awareness in the spirit world each soul is revealing itself in full and because of that is a more rounded and considerably larger being than it shows itself to be on earth.

There are many records of spirit communications which depict souls in spirit as being essentially no different in their thinking and behaviour than they were on earth. This is true to the extent and for as long as they remain earthbound.

Each soul in spirit, no longer constrained by a physical body with its brain and intelligence, and having thrown off the scales of unawareness and accepted itself fully, is a much more magnificent and glorious being than it can possibly appear to be while in the earth condition.

THE OVERSOUL – II

23rd – 26th February: I would like to develop the last session a little further.

The soul on earth is using the earth experience to concentrate on an aspect of itself while all its other aspects are, in a sense, waiting around. You have seen in other communications references to the oversoul sleeping while the soul is about its business. This is in essence the same idea with the proviso that there is no separation between the oversoul and the soul - they are one entity.

Now it seems that some clarification is needed as to how guides fit into the new picture I have painted. For instance, if you have a problem on which you meditate, could the suggested solution not equally well come from the dormant aspects of yourself – the oversoul, as it were – rather than from your guides?

Each soul has an inner knowing that there is more to it than it reveals at any given time to any person or group of people. Is that not so as far as you are concerned? That's what I was referring to when I said that the dormant aspects of the soul were always supportively in the background during an earth lifetime. But these aspects – the oversoul, if you like – are really and deliberately dormant while the particular life purpose on earth is being fulfilled or attempting to be fulfilled. If this were not so the whole purpose of the reincarnation might be nullified. Consider a physical analogy of one eye being covered up in order to allow the sight in the other to strengthen itself – although for the analogy to be a reasonably parallel one you would need to imagine a body with a minimum of fifty eyes with all of them covered up except one.

The image of the oversoul asleep is, in fact, a very helpful one.

While one aspect is being strengthened, the others are not in a position to influence, and perhaps retard by virtue of their overpowering presence, its development. One little eye might easily be neglected and allowed to weaken if, say, forty-nine others were beaming away all the time!

Thus what I have said in these last two sessions in no way cuts across anything I have said previously about the part guides play in the whole design.

I am aware that in some other spirit communications there is either no mention of guides or they are not classified as advanced souls in the way I have done. All souls in spirit either already know about the existence of guides or are so informed when they are ready to receive the information. They usually forget this when they are housed in physical bodies but they are reminded of it when the timing is right either while they are still on earth or afterwards. Whether they avail themselves of the help which guides have on offer is then, of course, entirely a matter for themselves.

There are many reasons why there is no mention of, or emphasis on, guides in some spirit communications. Some people like the idea of having guides, others don't. There are many roads to self-realisation or helping others towards self-realisation. None is necessarily the best one. The grand design accommodates all. I, and the others who are working with me on this venture, happen to think that the more souls are aware of the existence and avail themselves of the help of guides the easier will be the journey back to full awareness. They'll get there in the end anyway. As I have already said elsewhere, we are hoping that we can help to make the journey less painful.

THE OVERSOUL – III

28th February – 5th March: The concept of the soul as a many-sided structure which I discussed in the last two sessions should, I hope, be a source of encouragement (although I'm not too happy with the use of the word structure which implies rigidity; however, it serves for the purpose of illustration). Lack of progress in any one lifetime, although undesirable, is no tragedy since only one aspect of the soul is affected; all the other aspects are still in the bank, in a manner of speaking. Some people who believe in reincarnation worry in case that by using their free will in negative ways in a particular lifetime they will have nullified all the growth they may have achieved prior to that lifetime. There's no need for that worry as what's in the bank can't be touched during the lifetime in question.

For example, suppose we look again at the philosopher posited in the second last session. Assume that his latest lifetime was a litany of negativity. Thus he failed entirely to fulfil his life purpose and the aspect of soul which he had hoped to strengthen was, in fact, weakened. He will have to try again either through reincarnation or some other way, but the progress he has made in other areas is not diminished. His ultimate return to full awareness is delayed, of course, – his latest lifetime represents a regression to that extent.

Reincarnation would be a very problematical business indeed if the progress made by a soul prior to a physical lifetime were to be put at risk.

So now you're exercised about how you as a soul relate to you as oversoul. As always, we're faced with the consequences of trying to put a concept into words. As I have said already, soul and oversoul don't exist as separate entities. So you as you are now are also you as oversoul. It's just that there's a lot more to you than you think. It's as if you were a big mansion of which only one room is being used at present. That room was in a bit of a muddle and now you're getting it sorted out.

But, you say, maybe there are other rooms also in a muddle and you'll have to go through several incarnations or other undesirable processes in order to sort them out. This is an important point which may be best clarified by an example.

A soul reaches the second stage and is now once again exercising its free will. It has already got about half-way back to full awareness and has that much in the bank. It decides to incarnate as a human being. It has a lot to learn - or I should say, more correctly, to unlearn. It has no chance of fulfilling all its needs in one earth lifetime. With the help of guides it draws up a plan for an earth life designed to meet some of its needs. The life goes exactly as planned. It is reviewed with guides and the increase in the bank (the area of conscious mind) is observed A plan for a further earth life designed to eliminate more of its subconscious area of influence is drawn up. Once again the life is exactly as planned. Progress continues more or less according to plan through a number of earth lives with the proportion in the bank increasing all the time. Then things don't go as planned in one life. The particular areas of subconscious influence involved are not only not cleared but are reinforced. Subsequently it takes the soul two earth lives to clear them. This pattern is repeated in later lives. Eventually, however, the soul progresses beyond the second stage, although in doing so it has had to undertake many more earth experiences than would have been necessary had it managed to follow its plan fully in each earth life.

So – the position as to how many rooms in a mansion are still in a muddle varies with each mansion (soul). How to find out what your situation is? Just ask your guides and wait for the answer. However, I suggest that you decide whether you really want to know the answer or whether it would be in your best interests to know the answer before you ask the question.

HEALING – II

8th – 12th March: How far should one strive to overcome the limitations imposed by earth existence? If one chooses an environment and general situation in order to strengthen an aspect of soul, is there a risk that by evading those conditions (for example, through being healed of a bodily infirmity) one may be defeating one's life purpose?

Suppose that you find yourself in a position where it is open to you to develop a technique for easy and conscious astral travel or for healing illness through a form of mind control. What should your reaction be?

None of these things happens by accident. They are all fulfilling a part in the grand design. They are widening the range of opportunities for souls to increase their awareness. However, each soul has its own plan; what may be in accordance with one soul's plan may not fit in at all with another's. So the best answer I can give is that it is always in your best interests to check with your guides whether it is in accordance with your life plan for you to undertake any particular course of development which may come to your attention.

It is relevant to dwell for a little on the question of healing or prayer in relation to souls in spirit. In earlier sessions I have given my views on both healing and prayer and I don't propose to go over that ground again. However, I just wanted to comment a little further on some forms of healing, including prayer, directed expressly at souls who have left the earth scene.

On the one hand, this type of healing may be an expression of concern on the part of souls on earth for their fellow souls who are no longer physically with them. As such it may be a source of much comfort both to the healers and those whom they seek to heal.

On the other hand, it may be totally misdirected and thus create pressure and confusion for the recipient. A group of souls, say, projecting healing towards a soul without any knowledge of the spiritual needs of that soul may by the power of the thought forms with which they surround the soul propel it on a course of action or a line of thought detrimental to the working out of its own unique part in the grand design. People are acting for the best, of course, – usually – and out of real desire to help others but they have no concept of the harm they can do in finite terms by misguided acts of good works. I say in finite terms because, as I have already said elsewhere, the grand design is infinitely accommodating and adjusts itself automatically to any setback which occurs in each individual soul's plan. However, if only people on earth would have enough faith and trust to leave the operation of the grand design to those who designed and those who have agreed to operate it, much faster progress would be made, and there would be much less pain involved, in its implementation.

Now, as should be obvious from the thrust of our earlier sessions, I'm not suggesting for a minute that souls shouldn't help each other. Far from it. But if a person gives another person the sort of help he thinks that person needs he may not, in fact, be helping him at all. Or if he imposes his idea of help on another person against that person's will he is surely not helping him. What part does a desire for power or for recognition play in healing activities?

If you're involved in sending healing - through prayer or otherwise – to the physically dead, how do you know whether you're helping them or harming them? If you send loving thoughts to them, you're helping them; by loving thoughts I mean messages of goodwill which make no demands, not even to be reciprocated. Alternatively or additionally, if you ask your guides to convey to them your love and to help them in any way possible then, in my view, you're doing the very best you can for them. Ritualistic prayers for so-called suffering souls really only reinforce guilt in those souls if they already feel guilt;

the prayers make an assumption of the existence of sin so that feelings of guilt may very well be induced if they are not already present.

Some souls in spirit are in a state of suffering (as on earth) due to their own levels of unawareness. The souls who operate the grand design are constantly seeking opportunities to help them (without, of course, in any way imposing help). Sometimes these opportunities arise through the coordinated efforts of human beings and their guides (even though, in many instances, the human beings are not conscious of the assistance of guides). The most effective type of help is possible when all involved are working in harmony with consciousness of the part each plays in the work.

MIND CONTROL

10th – 19th April: We have discussed mind control to some extent in earlier sessions; at this stage I would like to say a little more on the subject.

As we saw in the development of the explanation of God, all creation, while having its own separate existence, still exists in the mind of its creator - or, more accurately, in its creator. The body owes its existence to the soul which is temporarily using it as a vehicle for an earth life. The soul designs the body along the lines which it considers best suited to its life purpose. The body doesn't have any motive force until the soul enters it and, of course, it loses that force and dies - or I should say is transformed - once the soul leaves it. It follows that the body is immobile without the soul which, as I have already explained, is synonymous with the mind. Accordingly, the influence of mind (soul) over matter (body) is total.

So when people talk about mind control what they are really discussing, albeit unconsciously for the most part, is the direction of mind control. It is there anyway; how it's being exercised is the only point in question.

As we have seen, the brain is the physical mechanism used by the mind (soul) in an earth life. Therefore, the agent of control in the physical sense is the brain. Thus a person in a coma, for example, where the brain has been rendered inoperative, is temporarily mindless in the physical sense – although, of course, his mind continues to function as soul.

The brain, being physical, is subject to physical conditioning. It is open to the influence of its environment and the ideas generally with which it comes into contact, including, of course, ideas about illness. For example, a child is taught that if he gets wet and wears wet clothes for any length of time he will catch a cold; if his conditioning has been successfully achieved, in other words if he believes what he's told, he will inevitably catch a cold.

What of a child that's born in a sickly condition – surely its brain has had no influence on that? Its brain, no; but itself (mind), yes – it chose that condition and presented itself with the challenge (or opportunity) of learning from it.

The mind feeds messages to the brain and gets messages back from it. That's how development (or otherwise) occurs during an earth lifetime. The only thing that matters in the long run is the impression created on the mind.

You feed the beliefs that you have about the aspect of yourself that reincarnated in your present physical body into your brain. Your brain in turn is receptive to conditioning in its earth environment and feeds further impressions into the mind which may change or reinforce its earlier beliefs. Thus does your body serve your mind through its physical agent, the brain; thus in reality does your body serve you; thus are the opportunities provided by earth existence put into effect.

A common form of conditioning, for instance, is that if a soul leaves its body in a state of sin it will go to Hell or certainly to some place of punishment whether temporary or eternal. The brain accepts the conditioning and relays it to the mind which enshrines it as one of its beliefs.

Another common form of conditioning is that a person needs six to eight hours sleep a night and that if he doesn't get that much sleep he'll feel tired the next day. So he will if he accepts the conditioning.

Now suppose that you experience some physical symptoms which suggest to you that you are unwell or malfunctioning in some way; for example, your eyes feel strained. The expected reaction in your environment is to have your eyes tested and as a result you will probably find yourself wearing glasses. The sequence is logical; your eyes feel strained, therefore you need to have them tested, you are supplied with glasses, and you believe from then on that your eyes are defective.

But, you say, the test showed that they were defective; that's a physical fact. Yes, and the provision of glasses will ensure that they remain defective. (I want to make dear that I'm not making any judgment about eye-tests or any other kinds of tests, or remedial practices such as wearing glasses; if wearing glasses helps people to have better vision, then the practice has its own merit; in the physical sense it can obviously, and in the spiritual sense it can possibly, be helpful if a natural faculty is aided by artificial means.)

The advances made in this century in medical technology - as indeed in technology generally - have, ironically, reduced people's dependence on themselves. Even the most minor illnesses are now treated with drugs of various kinds. The result is, of course, that the remedial properties built into the design of the body are being destroyed. In physical terms it's a classic example of creation turning on its creator. (Again I have to say that I'm making no judgment on technology in itself; it has its own important part to play in the grand design.)

To return to the example of the defective eyes - what alternative is there to the provision of glasses if the person's visual capacity is to be improved? The common belief is that there's no alternative. For a person who accepts that belief there is, in fact, no alternative. But the reality is that most illnesses or physical defects can be cured by the mind working through the brain.

The first step is to accept that it can be done; full acceptance is not easy because of the prevailing beliefs in many communities. The next step is for the mind to transmit its belief to the body through the brain and to do it repeatedly. If there is one particular area of the body – say the eyes again – which seems to be defective, I suggest that a phrase such as – 'my eyes are perfect' – repeated for approximately five minutes each day for about fifty days *with full acceptance that the eyes are perfect though not at present manifesting their perfection* will produce apparently miraculous results. The same type of formula can, of course, be used for any other part of the body. No, I haven't forgotten - before doing any exercise of this kind it would be advisable to confirm from your guides that it wouldn't adversely affect your life purpose in any way.

The body starts out with all the ingredients needed for the mind's purpose. Its life-span is pre-ordained by the mind. Subject to the overriding priority of its life purpose it is in the mind's best interests that the body should operate to its full potential. Therefore the mind's beliefs about the body and its own relationship with and influence over the body are important towards the fulfilment of its life purpose.

In what I'm saying in this session I'm seeking to help souls to accept and fulfil the full potential of their earth experiences. If they have difficulty about such acceptance it is better for them to stay with the traditional practices for as long as they find them supportive. Ultimately, in any case, they will come to an acceptance of the magnitude of their being - only the road will be longer and their feet will be more blistered, metaphorically speaking.

PHYSICAL CONFLICT

5th – 8th May: "There will be wars and rumours of wars" was a safe prophecy if ever there was one. Physical conflict of one kind or another has been a constant feature of human existence. Except in comparatively rare instances people have not been given to eating each other (physically!), but in most other ways many of them behave towards each other, through the abuse of free will, in a much less civilised way than non-humans do.

Basically, as I've said before, it's a question of non-awareness.

Only an unaware soul can treat another soul, whether in a physical environment or not, with lack of respect. At the same time it's not a black and white matter. As we saw in earlier sessions, the growth of awareness may very well be helped by extremely unaware behaviour. In that sense, physical conflict, including war, may serve a spiritual purpose – which, of course, is not the purpose the participants see or intend.

Suppose somebody is about to attack you physically what should you do? You have only three obvious options - accept the attack passively, run away if you can, or fight back. If you are spiritually aware, what do you think you should do?

You have other options which are not so obvious. Bearing in mind that he is an unaware soul or he wouldn't be on the point of assaulting you, you could send him love, you could try to hold his eyes with yours, you could call on him to stop, and you could try to reason with him. I suggest that all of these options should be tried, and they can be done instantaneously. If they all fail, the best thing to do, in my view, is to follow your feelings in as detached a way as you can. Your feelings (the real you) will tell you the best way to cope with the situation. This may turn out to be the use of physical force to whatever extent is required. Is that not an interference with his free will? No, it's presenting him with a consequence of his act of free will. He is encroaching on your "space", imposing or seeking to impose his will on yours; he has to learn not to do this. It may be that he will not begin to learn it unless the lesson is sharply administered.

You find it somewhat surprising that I'm justifying the use of physical force in certain circumstances. To be accurate, I'm not actually justifying it - I'm saying positively that it may be the best option in some situations. It's important to remember that what matters is the spiritual effect, not the physical one.

So – what about wars? One can reason from the particular to the general. Wars usually start because one country or group of countries seeks to impose its will on another. Again, if all other options fail, the use of physical force in self-defence may spiritually be the best means of dealing with the situation.

Does all this presuppose, then, that individuals or groups or nations or alliances of nations should in their best spiritual interests seek to increase their capacity for self-defence? If it doesn't, what's the point of saying that self-defence by the use of physical force may be the best option in certain circumstances?

It's relevant to indulge in what may seem to be a digression but isn't really, since you have just communicated your concern that you should record accurately what I am transmitting to you. A thought even flashed through your mind that some other soul may have temporarily taken over the "controls". Remember my suggestion that in order to improve and preserve the quality of communication with your guides you should ask them not to let any other soul come through to you except by arrangement? The point I'm making now is not that having done this no other soul can now come through to you except with your agreement (which is the position) but that you are, in fact, defending yourself and your own "space" in this way by the best means open to you. Each soul's piece of the jig-saw is its own sacred preserve and it is in its best spiritual interests to keep it so as it is in the best interests of each and every other soul that they should be prevented from intruding on it.

The distinction in terms of awareness is between aggression and self-defence. Aggression in the sense of imposition or attempted imposition of one will on another is always an expression of unawareness. Self-defence for as long as it is strictly confined to the prevention of aggression is an expression of awareness. How about the defence of others from aggression? For your answer may I again refer you to the example of guides. Out of respect for free will they will only intervene if asked to do so. I cannot give you any better guideline than that.

Yes, but suppose an old lady is being mugged; a passer-by will not know whether she is asking for help or not. In the case of physical aggression such as mugging it is always reasonable to assume that the victim is asking for help although perhaps not in a position to articulate the request; any passer-by who does not try to help the victim is ignoring a valuable opportunity for spiritual growth; this applies equally whether the victim of assault is human or non-human.

In the case of mental or spiritual aggression - brain-washing, for example, - the victim may not wish, or be ready, to accept help. It would be an interference with his free will to impose, or try to impose, help on him. I include prayer and spiritual healing in the category of interference. In due course he will become aware that help is available to him in many different forms; one form will appeal to him, he will ask for it in his own way and he will be ready to receive maximum benefit from it.

Now to answer the questions asked five paragraphs ago; if there seems to be a threat of aggression against them the answer is yes. The second question doesn't arise. Of course, there wouldn't even be a threat of aggression if all humans had increased their awareness to the point where they saw each person's free will as sacrosanct; but then physical existence on earth would no longer be necessary.

Where does all this leave campaigns for nuclear disarmament, etc.?
To the extent that they are seeking an end to aggression on a global scale they are helpful in the spiritual sense.

What about the Christian message of turning the other cheek?

This can be a most effective method of self-defence as long as the person using it remains free in his feelings and thoughts - for example, if he does not harbour resentment or hatred. The effect on the aggressor may turn out to be profound.

The physical means used to prevent aggression are spiritually of no consequence or relative importance in themselves. Their only significance is in the effect which they produce both in the aggressor and the recipient of his aggression.

EUTHANASIA: SUICIDE

11th – 14th May: I have to keep on saying things like - "as we have already seen" or "as I explained in earlier sessions" because each new session is in some way a development of material given earlier. So I hope you'll bear with the repetition.

Well, as we have already seen(!), each soul, in conjunction with its guides – if it decides to have guides – designs its physical existence, including the timing of the birth and death of its body. This raises questions such as, for instance, how euthanasia and suicide fit into the design, if they do.

There is one clear distinction between euthanasia and suicide, which is that euthanasia is performed by somebody else whereas suicide is self-operated. Euthanasia may, of course, be performed as a result of an earlier request by the person concerned but essentially that is suicide.

Euthanasia, in the sense of an act performed - usually with altruistic motivation - by another or others on a person without the consent of that person, is an interference with free will and, accordingly, falls into the category of unawareness. For that reason I don't intend to dwell on it any further.

Suicide, in the sense of an act voluntarily performed by a person on himself, is an expression of free will and, accordingly, may fall into either category (of awareness or unawareness). Every human being commits suicide in one way or another.

The thrust of traditional teaching in this area is that God creates each soul and each body and that only God has the right to decide the timing and the manner of the birth and death of each body. However, once you accept that each soul is a part of God you can look on the matter from a different viewpoint. Once you further accept that each soul designs its own body and its own life on earth before it enters into the body your whole perspective is changed. Now you are the creator. (And, of course, it is still true to say that God is the creator in that you are part of God, but obviously it's an inadequate and misleading version of truth once it's expressed without elaboration.)

When I say that every human being commits suicide in one way or another, I'm thinking firstly of the fact that each soul's life plan comprehends the birth and death of the body which it has designed for a projected earth existence, and secondly of the fact that the plan also comprehends the manner of that birth and death. The plan in one case may envisage death by means of a heart attack, in another through a form of cancer, in another by way of a car crash, in another through an overdose of sleeping pills, and so on. The important thing to bear in mind is that the manner of death of the body is determined in the soul's pre-earth-existence life plan. However, as has been outlined in earlier sessions, the plan is not always adhered to and many of what are commonly termed suicides are more likely to be deviations from than adherence to plan; for example, when they are committed in unbalanced (e.g., depressive) states of mind.

It is a very unwise exercise for any person to pass judgment on another because of that person's manner of death - indeed, of course, to pass judgment for any reason. Each soul's plan is specially designed to cater for its needs, and even if it deviates from it the grand design will adjust itself to the deviation(s) and eventually all will be well for that soul. So do not grieve for anybody who commits suicide in a more obvious way than others in his community; and, above all, don't waste your energy and in the process retard your own development by making, and perhaps acting on, assumptions about his eternal future.

Is it advisable to try to find out what manner of death one has chosen? Usually, no. It is easier for people to fulfil their life purpose if they live in the present. The knowledge of when and how they were going to die would be likely to be a constraining burden for most people to carry. The lessons of each day have more impact if its experiences are not foreseen. This, after all, is why the grand design provided that people would not remember their plans while on earth.

SEX

17th – 28th May: In an earlier session I discussed the relative positions of the spiritual and the material in the overall scheme of things. In summary, my conclusion was that the material was an aid to the spiritual and not to be regarded as separate from it.

Possibly the most central and confused area in this context is that of physical relations between the sexes. On the one hand, there's a widely held view that promiscuity in sexual matters is a barrier to growth in spirituality, and there's a less widely held view that any indulgence at all in sexual activity is detrimental to spirituality. On the other hand, strong arguments are put forward for achieving freedom and/or spirituality through the release of the body from its sexual inhibitions.

The human body was blueprinted in male and female forms not alone for obvious reproductive reasons but also as a means of achieving growth in awareness through inter and contrasting relationships. That there should be physical attraction between the sexes was an integral part of the blueprint.

Society, in particular western society, is ordered in such a way that a man and a woman are, generally speaking, expected to be exclusive in their behaviour; for example, if married, they should neither desire (at least obviously!) nor have sexual relations with anybody except each other; if single, they are expected to be faithful to one person (at least at a time!); if attached to a religious order which has a rule of celibacy, they are forbidden to indulge in any sexual activity. The difficulty, then, facing both sexes is that they have inbuilt natural urges which they must restrain if they are not to be ostracised or condemned in some way by society.

It is interesting to look at sexual mores in the context of the different stages of evolutionary growth as I have outlined them. At the first - non-human - stage the natural urges are followed with, for the most part, no exclusivity. At the second - human - stage exclusivity enters and there is restraint on the natural urges. After the second stage there is no longer sex differentiation - the division into male and female has served its purpose.

Sexual relations at the first stage tend to be direct and uncomplicated although they are preceded by mating rituals in some instances. At the second stage a greater degree of sophistication is generally sought and physical demonstrations of affection and communication, such as hugging, kissing, touching, are practised both as incidental to explicitly sexual relationships and to relationships between members of families and between friends and acquaintances. At the other stages the physical element is no longer present, but love is demonstrated in non-exclusive, more continuous, stronger and more pleasurable ways than is possible at the second stage. The best description I can give is that there is a fusion of being. By that I don't mean that any soul loses its individuality, even momentarily. There is a totality of understanding and of oneness of communication and of feeling (being) which is all the more comprehensive because of the consciousness of individuality which remains ever-present. If, say, I merge into you (on the assumption that that could happen - which it couldn't) communication between us is no longer possible. But if you and I can achieve a form of communication where the love that we are simply manifests itself towards each other through our being with total openness and awareness of what we are, without the necessity for any type of camouflage or ritual and without any possibility of misunderstanding of any kind, then that is a state of perfect harmony which is a source of the greatest possible sharing of pleasure for both of us.

The only reason for the existence of the physical is so that it will serve as a means of helping spirit beings raise their levels of awareness. Accordingly, if the physical is not used for spiritual purposes there is a waste of opportunity for growth. Translated into sexual terms this means that it is likely that promiscuous behaviour, in the sense of obsession with the performance of the sexual act whether with another or others, is more of a hindrance than a help towards awareness (which, of course, applies to all obsessions).

There are many ways of arriving at the same end (increased awareness), no one of them necessarily better than another. In sexual matters, as with all others, it is most important (a) to respect absolutely the free will of each person and its need to have its own "space", and (b) to be free of all obsessions.

Now, again drawing attention to the fact that there are many ways towards increased awareness and that my way is only one of those, I feel it incumbent on me to give my suggestions which I hope will be of help in this basic and complex area of human relations.

For a start, I would not recommend over-indulgence in sexual activity, not because I see it in black and white terms of right and wrong but because it leads to dependence and obsessiveness.

Neither would I recommend sexual activity at all for its own sake, e.g., as a means of physical release; if a person uses it for that purpose he will find himself increasingly dependent on it. By and large, the exclusivity which obtains in sexual activity is spiritually helpful in that with time it compels a reappraisal of values and physical expression becomes less significant; in other words, physical attraction is not of predominant or unbalanced importance. In eternal terms this is very important since the physical has no part to play after the second stage and life on earth is intended as a preparation for moving into the third stage and beyond it. I know that there is a common belief that frustration, with all sorts of attendant problems, results from non-indulgence in sexual activity. Of course, it is only the belief which causes the problems (as you will remember from our recent session on mind control); all frustrations are products of the mind.

Just as I don't recommend sexual activity for its own sake neither do I recommend celibacy for its own sake. If undertaken as a means of mortifying the flesh or if it is in any way perceived as a penance or a deprivation it is likely to be detrimental to spiritual advancement.

Obsessiveness takes many forms. In sexual terms it can include fear of sexual expression as well as dependence of it. So, in one case, the solution from a spiritual point of view may lie in transforming this fear into love through, for example, a loving sexual relationship and, in the other, in reducing the level of sexual activity or perhaps becoming celibate, at least for a time.

So far I have outlined what I don't recommend. It's time for me to say what I do recommend. I think the clearest thing I can do is to list my recommendations and incidental comments, as follows:

1.   If possible, study all our previous sessions but particularly those relating to God, feeling and emotion, freedom, free will, how the world came into being, the stages of evolutionary growth, reincarnation, the significance of the body within the spiritual continuity of life, and the mind (soul) with particular reference to the relationship between the mind and the body.

2.   Having studied the sessions you can now understand and accept, I hope, that life is a spiritual reality, that physical life has no real meaning except in a spiritual context, that ultimately the only significance of the physical is as an aid or a vehicle for the spiritual and that there is no separation between them, and, finally, that the physical (matter) is entirely subject to the control of the spiritual (mind).

3.   Consequently, if you concentrate on the physical or material in isolation from its spiritual importance you are separating yourself from yourself - in reality behaving unnaturally – and you will neither be able to find inner harmony nor make spiritual progress until you realise and accept this.

4.   Physical demonstrations of love are not only desirable but necessary in certain relationships, e.g., parents and children, but they are no substitute for true spiritual love which does not need to be physically expressed. Indeed, love which demands physical expression is likely to be emotion rather than feeling.

5.   Ideally, marital relationships – or similar types of relationships –

should outgrow physical needs – in other words, sexual intercourse should be an experience of joyful spirituality which incorporates physical release – to allow both partners to free themselves from any emotional obsessions and to express themselves spiritually (i.e. fully) towards each other and towards all others with whom they come into contact.

6. In case of misunderstanding, I want to elaborate on what I have said at 4 above in order to make dear that I am not advocating abandonment during a physical lifetime of physical demonstrations of love. What I am trying to get across is that such demonstrations cannot of themselves provide spiritual freedom. This can only be achieved when feeling (as I have described it in an earlier session) replaces emotion (as I have described it in the same session). Feeling is a matter of being, not demonstration; lack of demonstration does not necessarily imply aware or unaware expression of feeling; on the other hand, shows of demonstration do not necessarily imply aware or unaware expression of feeling, either. How feeling manifests itself is entirely an individual matter. However, I must add that, since the physical is an aid to the spiritual, it is a wonderful bonus when the body can be freely (i.e., non-obsessively) used in loving relationship, which of course, includes sexual relationship.

7. In its ultimate state of awareness the soul is complete in itself and does not need anything. At the same time, it is one with all other souls and relates to them in total harmony of communication. The communication has a different form of expression geared to each soul with each soul automatically knowing how to communicate with each other soul without any invasion of "space" by an unwelcome intrusion.

8. Whatever road you choose to travel on your way back to full awareness you need to bear in mind that you cannot get back to that state without freeing yourself completely from even the minutest form of obsession. Obviously it is a great step forward if you can succeed in doing this to a significant extent while still surrounded by powerful sources of obsession, as happens on earth – which is what makes life on earth such a marvellous

learning experience.

9. Joy is a central attribute of spirit so ideally life on earth and all its physical accompaniments and arrangements should be a source of joy. The physical circumstances which give rise to joy change or are differently perceived as awareness increases; difficulties may occur in relationships if this is not understood. Ultimately, each person must come to terms with the fact that his brief stay on earth is an opportunity which he has chosen primarily for his own spiritual growth – not anybody else's. Of course, if he can help others to grow too, that's great – and, needless to say, the more he grows, the more he can help.

POLITICS

10th – 14th June: On the face of it, it may be somewhat surprising that I should consider politics as a subject for discussion. I think it desirable that I should do so since the business of politics affects the day to day living of people to a significant extent in one way or another.

In the modem world the process of government has largely evolved from imperial and monarchical systems to democracies of various kinds. The transition has been from government by acquisition or inheritance to election or selection from amongst the people themselves. Imperial and monarchical systems recognised and indeed promoted inequalities - for instance, through the establishment of different classes of nobility. In a democracy all the people have equal rights (in theory, at least!).

As you would expect, the evolution of governmental systems is in accordance with the grand design and shows that, in spite of all the pronouncements and apparent indications to the contrary (including two world wars already in this century), much progress has been made in the implementation of the design. In human terms the emphasis on the value of the individual and respect for the individual has never been greater than it is today.

The movement towards democracy is, in fact, a reflection of the movement towards the seventh and ultimate stage of awareness. The seventh stage is an ideal form of democracy. Whereas in the human condition there are governments and laws and people placed in positions of authority over others, which to some extent negates the idea of equality, at the seventh stage there is absolute equality and there is no need for any of these restrictions.

Politics, in the democratic sense, has come to be regarded as an activity in which people engage in order to get themselves or others elected as public representatives and thus into a position to regulate the business of government. There are, of course, different levels of engagement in politics. At the lowest or minimum level are the people whose activity is confined to voting in elections. Then there are those who seek the assistance of public representatives either for personal or community purposes. There are the people behind the scenes, the back-room workers, the canvassers of votes, the financial supporters, who stay out of the limelight themselves but who do all in their power to get particular persons or parties elected to representative office. There are the people who seek, or allow themselves to be selected for, representative positions. And, ultimately, there are the people who become the leaders or the government.

Needless to say, the democratic system in its human context provides many learning opportunities from a spiritual point of view. The person who is obsessed with power gets much scope to free himself from his obsession. So does the person who craves for recognition, as does the person who thinks he knows what's best for others, or the person who needs to be occupied all the time, or the person who hates being alone, or the person who is driven by missionary fervour in the service of others.

As a person becomes more aware he will find himself less inclined to become involved in political activity. He will see that the management of people's affairs is primarily a matter for themselves and that it is their right to be allowed to develop in their own way - which doesn't, of course, preclude their being helped, if they so wish. A person who is actively involved in politics is continually seeking to impress on others his point of view or the point of view of his party. His actions in favour of one person may well obstruct another's opportunity.

But, you object, somebody has to run a country or a community; somebody has to make laws and see that they are observed – otherwise there will be chaos. Yes, unfortunately, that is still the position. While it remains so – and it will until each person has total respect for the free will of all others and has absolute tolerance of them and acceptance of their equality in God with him – the earth experiment, or something similar, will continue to be needed.

Well, then, as a person gains awareness how does he live with the system as it is? By keeping himself free as far as he can in his feelings and thoughts, by sharing those feelings and thoughts – without in any way seeking to impose them – with others when suitable opportunities to do so occur, and by helping in that way to create more accepting and tolerant communities in which souls will have freedom to expand their consciousness. A restricted, narrow-minded community is like a garden where the flowers are stunted by weeds and thorn bushes, whereas a liberal, open-minded community is like a garden where the flowers bloom in the sun with nothing to inhibit their growth.

Does the practice of politics not give a readymade and in many ways ideal platform for the sharing of feelings and thoughts? In my view, no. Politics is a competitive business. One politician is successful only at the expense of another. He is concerned to establish that his thoughts and actions are superior to those of another or others. It is difficult for him to be sincere with himself or with others. He is, in practice, at all times making a plea for recognition and if his plea is not successful he doesn't get elected to representative office. To the aware person recognition doesn't count. He manifests himself as he is; how others react to him is exclusively their affair.

While politicians give public expression to a craving for recognition such craving is common in varying degrees to human beings generally. Politics and politicians play their own part in the grand design – in a more public and dramatic way than most others. Politicians as a group are likely to be neither more nor less aware than the majority of the people whom they represent; they are, in fact, likely to mirror the state of awareness of the community which they represent.

One final thought; there's a big difference between sharing your thoughts with others and seeking to influence others to your way of thinking. I might have said that there was all the difference in the world but it would be more accurate to say that there's a world of awareness in the difference.

ACTIVITY

20th June – 9th July: Activity of one kind or another is common to all souls. It is not possible to be and not be active. The soul is in fact always active even when it is using a physical body and even when that body is asleep.

The soul is feeling and feeling is active; it is eternally creative by thought, word and deed. Paradoxically, its greatest creativity is likely to be when the body is still or apparently passive.

In this session I mean activity to include work in the sense in which I think work is commonly understood - that which people do in order to earn money or keep house so that they can provide the necessities and luxuries of physical living for themselves and their families.

By and large, work is generally perceived to be a form of slavery. It is exceptional for people to find jobs which give them satisfaction on a continuing basis.

Yet workplaces provide other forms of satisfaction; for example, companionship, a sense of belonging, a feeling of compatibility with others, status, fulfilment of ambition.

In modern times technology, particularly computers, is taking over much of the work previously performed manually. This is making life easier, on the one hand, but is increasing unemployment on the other. Many people are now coming on the job market whose prospects of ever getting continuous employment or even any employment at all are slim. So, since a reversion to pre-computer practices is unlikely, people are faced with a double challenge of accepting a lower standard of living and of arriving at a new perception of work and of leisure which will have the effect of making both more enjoyable and productive.

You may remember that I said some time ago that spiritually no particular activity has of itself greater value than another. An activity acquires value from its effect on the person who performs it. One man will get great value from a particular type of work, whereas another will find it boring and frustrating. One person will get agitated and suffer sleepless nights over work problems; another will take similar problems in his stride and see them as challenges to be faced and enjoyed.

A common example of frustration is that of a person who is employed in what to him seems to be a dull, routine job and who feels that he has missed out, or is missing out, on opportunities to do something meaningful with his life. Here again the separation between the spiritual and material becomes apparent; for instance, charitable or missionary activity assumes an aura of importance which is not perceived in a routine clerical job.

Unfortunately, I can't wave a magic wand and take the slavery out of work although I have tried to show ways of doing this in earlier sessions, particularly the one on freedom. If people can accept that before they were born they chose the environment and the work most suited to the achievement of their particular life purpose it should be easier for them to reconcile themselves to their jobs and to begin to look on them in a different light and hopefully to see that their only missed opportunity is in their attitude to their jobs.

This is a subject which is of more than passing interest to you personally. You work at a job and in your spare time you do what might be loosely described as counselling (including these sessions). From the spiritual point of view you see your voluntary activity as being the much more important and you would wish to be in a position financially to do it full time.

Two questions arise; is, in fact, your work as important for you spiritually as your voluntary activity?; and how can the only importance spiritually of your voluntary activity lie in its effect on yourself?

Now I have to remind you that you chose your work. There were certain lessons which you wanted to learn in this lifetime and which you could best learn in the type of work and environment in which you operate. Once you have learned these lessons it will no longer be necessary for you to continue with that work. So the answer to your first question is that at the present time your work is just as important for you spiritually as your voluntary activity. In fact, one complements the other in helping you fulfil your life purpose.

You can readily appreciate the effect of these sessions on yourself.
But how can that be their only importance spiritually? Surely by encouraging you to write down all this material I am assigning importance to the material not just for you but for others? It is certainly my hope and the hope of the others who have joined with me on this project that many people will read and be helped by your record of our sessions. But the reading of it becomes their activity; and for them the only importance spiritually of that reading will be its effect on themselves. If what you are writing now is never published or nobody but yourself ever reads it you can see that your activity in receiving and writing it can have no importance spiritually except in its effect on you. If it is published, people will have to decide for themselves whether to read it or not; that is their effort, their activity, and the effect of the reading will be different for each individual.

Similarly, in the other counselling which you do you act as a channel for spirit and you convey information and suggestions to people which you hope will be helpful to them. What you do and how you do it has objective and absolute importance for yourself; but even though you may approach each session in exactly the same way the value which your listeners get is entirely relative to each of them. Their decisions, firstly in asking for your help, secondly in listening and how they listen, and thirdly in how they respond, are their own activities and have spiritual importance only for themselves.

You are still not satisfied. You argue that if a book is read by, say, a million people and most of them are helped in some way by it doesn't that make the book important in itself? You forget - I was talking about activity. The book is a product of activity and it is an instrument of activity for as long as it is being read but it just lies there until somebody chooses to read it and then the effect it produces is entirely a matter for that person. In itself a book has whatever importance a person or people assign to it.

Now, you see, I have made a distinction between the fruit of a person's activity, e.g., a book, and the activity itself, e.g., the writing of a book. The actual outcome of the writing (the book) has relative importance for each of its readers and is important in itself for that reason, but its readers' activity in reading it is of importance spiritually only in its effect on themselves.

All this may sound rather abstruse so perhaps two illustrations may help.

A man works for most of his life in a routine, apparently unimportant, job. He's a cheerful, happy man, who brings his disposition to bear on his job and the whole environment in which he lives and works.

Another man is a highly successful writer. His books are generally acknowledged to be opinion-shapers towards a liberalisation of attitudes. Yet he himself is discontented with the pace of change and he manifests that discontent in the environment in which he operates.

Objectively, it is probably true that the body of work which the second man has created has more accrued importance than that of the first. Yet it is also probably true that from a spiritual point of view the first man has gained more from his activity than the second man.

In both cases the only importance of their activities lies in their effects on themselves. The results of their activities may have relative importance for other people but again the scale of that importance is determined by their own activities in responding to those results.

It would be a useful exercise for a person to list the lessons or the learning experiences which he feels his work has offered him from a spiritual point of view and then to evaluate his response to those lessons or experiences.

DEATH – WHAT HAPPENS?

8th – 9th July: In the session on the second stage of evolutionary growth I outlined in a broad way what happens when a soul leaves its physical body. Obviously, the circumstances in which a soul finds itself on transition vary with each individual soul and depend on its state (of mind) at the time of the death of the body.

Take the case of a man who dies believing that there's nothing beyond the death of the body. He is convinced that he is still alive on earth and even though he sees his body being buried or cremated he thinks that a horrible mistake has been made. He stays around his relatives and friends trying to get somebody to listen to him. He can't understand why he's not getting through to them. He sees them grieving for him and talking about him as if he were dead. It's a time of much confusion for him.

Meanwhile, souls in spirit, including his guide or guides (if he had agreed to have any for his earth lifetime), are trying to help him. While he's in a state of confusion and single-minded concentration on trying to get somebody on earth to listen to him it is unlikely that the other souls will be able to get through to him; in any event, they will probably feel that he's not yet ready to accept his present state. Since he's no longer bound by time in the same way as on earth he's not conscious of the passage of time. In earth terms his confusion may even cover a period of years, but while that sounds bad to somebody on earth it's not so bad in the spirit sense. The closest analogy I can give is that of a person who is concussed who is not aware of what is going on around him and yet who continues with what he was doing before he became concussed though he will have no recollection of this later nor will he have any idea of how long he was concussed.

Ultimately the souls who are waiting to help get their opportunity.

The most likely way for this to happen is through a soul who was either a relative or a friend of his while on earth. His concentration on the earth scene will slacken at some stage and the other soul chooses this opportunity to bring itself to his attention. Once he accepts that he has, in fact, died in the physical sense but that he is still alive in reality and that life is a continuity he is on the road to adjustment to his new condition and there are many souls available to help him according to his capacity to receive help.

People who have no belief in life after death are in the most difficult condition of all in so far as adjustment to life in spirit is concerned. That's why acceptance of the continuity of life is the most basically advantageous condition for any soul.

The next most difficult condition is where a person has totally inflexible beliefs about life in spirit - for example, if he believes that after death he will be judged by God and consigned to a place of reward or punishment maybe for eternity or maybe until a final Day of Judgment when his body will be miraculously rejoined with his soul to experience an eternity of Heaven or Hell. He may well continue to be limited by those beliefs for a long time until he begins to wonder why things aren't happening the way he expected they would or perhaps until his association with other souls who may have started to change their beliefs may also bring him to question his beliefs.

The best condition of all in which to make the transition is one of complete acceptance of the continuity of life, of individual responsibility for spiritual development and of the fact that there are many evolved souls only waiting to be asked for help. A soul leaving its body in that frame of mind will make rapid progress through the stages back to full awareness. The shuttered mind is the most impenetrable barrier of all against spiritual progress.

How can people best help their friends or relatives or acquaintances who have died, or indeed the "dead" generally? If you remember, I already gave my view on this in our sessions on prayer -

that is, that the best way to help is by asking your guides to convey your concern and love to them and to suggest to them that the guides will provide all the help they need if they are prepared to accept such help; the guides will find the most suitable opportunity to do this.

I can only recommend the way that seems best and simplest to me.

Others use different ways, including prayer. Although they may succeed I personally wouldn't recommend any way other than the one I have outlined. I'll try to explain why.

If, say, a group of individuals pray to God for a particular soul their thoughts are concentrated on that soul while they are praying and presumably they are asking that it should be granted eternal happiness. It is unlikely that any two of them will have coinciding views as to what constitutes eternal happiness. All those thoughts form a powerful pressure around the soul and because the thoughts are more than likely in conflict with each other (for example, in their conception of eternal happiness) the pressure may be extremely inharmonious, thus causing much confusion in the recipient (or victim!). The prayers may succeed in that the pressure may become so unbearable that the soul has to seek help - but I'm sure it's not the wish of those praying that their prayers should be answered in that way.

Prayer isn't, of course, the only method used by people for trying to help the dead. Groups of people come together and invite earthbound souls to communicate with them so that they can talk to them and advise them. Individuals and groups also use other methods, such as ouija boards or séances or mediumistic communication. All of these methods may be helpful but unless they are guided and controlled by evolved souls they may also be harmful – for instance, by giving unaware souls free rein to act mischievously even to the extent sometimes of pretending to be relatives or friends of the people attempting communication.

Souls are sometimes referred to as being trapped, e.g., in a belief that they are still alive on earth, and there is a school of thought that because these souls are earthbound they can only be directly helped by people on earth. You have come across a recent example of this where a soul in spirit apparently used the body of a medium in order to enable a trapped soul to speak to a human being and thus receive help. I regret to say that this was not a genuine experience. It does not - and cannot - happen that a soul who is prepared to accept help can't be helped, and isn't helped, solely from spirit sources. You may remember that at one stage I talked about awareness as a ladder with help continuously flowing downwards from the top to the bottom. The realms of possibility expand as a soul climbs the ladder. At the top everything is possible - which, of course, means that nothing is impossible. So while sometimes it may be convenient for souls in spirit to use humans to help them to help souls who are having difficulty adjusting to changed conditions - and this is probably done as a means of helping the humans also - it isn't necessary for them to do so.

In a sense every soul who has not yet regained full awareness is trapped in its feeling and thinking. However, no soul is ever abandoned; the grand design has seen to that. Help is provided when the time is right without any interference with free will. Nobody can free a trapped soul but itself. When it accepts the help available to it is on the road to freedom. Anybody who claims that he frees trapped souls   is   simply   deluding   himself   and/or   others.

COMMUNICATION WITH SPIRIT

14th – 17th July: In the last session I expressed regret that a particular experience was not genuine. In case of misunderstanding I want to make it clear that my regret was because of the delusion – needless to say, I don't regret that souls aren't trapped in the sense described.

As you know, the difficulty about communication between souls temporarily in human form and other souls is that the others can't readily be seen. Because of this humans are at a disadvantage in deciding whether apparent communications are products of their own subconscious or are genuine communications from spirit and, if genuine, whether the interpretation or wording given to them is accurate.

It is, of course, part of the grand design that humans should not generally be aware of other souls around them; they are on earth to benefit from the human experience, which means limiting themselves to the constraints of earth and in trying to overcome them to learn whatever lessons they need to learn. The ideal thing, in my view, is to be able to combine unobtrusive communication (e.g., with guides) with day-to-day living so that one blends with the other and helps with it.

Some people make communication with "the spirit world" part of their daily living so that it becomes their work. They will, of course, have chosen to do this before coming on earth and will have specially prepared their bodies in order to facilitate communication. They are commonly called mediums. There are different forms of mediumship, such as trance, or inspirational, or automatic writing. In trance mediumship the human agent seems to be in a trance while a soul or souls in spirit apparently use his voice-box. In inspirational mediumship the human agent receives thoughts or impressions from a soul or souls in spirit and puts his own interpretation and words on them. With automatic writing the human agent merely allows his hand to be used and is unconscious of what is being produced.

The first point I want to make is predictable and is one that the reader of the record of these sessions is probably tired of seeing repeated. It is, of course, that any person who is involved in mediumship of any kind should make sure to ask his guides to control the flow of communication. Otherwise he is likely to find himself in the business of self-delusion and of deluding others no matter how sincere he may be about what he's trying to do.

You may remember that in our session on possession I said that it wasn't possible for any soul to take over the body of another even if the human were willing to allow that to happen. So in trance mediumship the human's body is not taken over by a soul in spirit. What happens is that a form of self-hypnosis takes place. The mediums for whatever reason don't have the courage to admit even to themselves that what's really happening is that thoughts are being impressed on their minds and that they are relaying those thoughts; in other words, while they express their willingness to participate in the events by freely donating the use of their bodies they are at the same time afraid of that participation in some way; so they sidestep their fear by convincing themselves, even to the extent of changing completely their vocal form of expression, that spirit beings are temporarily using their bodies. This doesn't necessarily in any way take from the validity of the communications which they transmit. It's just a fact that there's no difference between trance and inspirational mediumship in so far as the actual method of transmission is concerned. Automatic writing is different in that all that's involved is willingness on the human's part to allow his hand to be moved over a sheet of paper; he can, of course, stop the movement at any time.

Anybody who chooses to be a medium takes on a big responsibility. If he misleads himself or allows himself to be misled he is living a lie which will add to the debt he owes himself as a part

PADDY MCMAHON

of God. Because he has no way of proving whether much of the information he gets is true or false he has no way of avoiding being misled unless he takes the precaution of having his communications controlled by an evolved soul or souls. Having taken that precaution he can then rely absolutely on the validity of the communications he receives from spirit sources. He may still have difficulties of interpretation but this is part of his own learning experience and should naturally become less and less with experience in direct proportion to the thoroughness with which he learns from experience.

I strongly recommend that all communications which purport to come from spirit, whether they come directly or through a medium, should be tested for genuineness. This can best be done through guides.

In your own case you want to apply the test to what you have written in these sessions. Since from an early stage in your conscious communication with spirit you asked that all further communication should be controlled by your guides you need have no doubts whatever about the validity or genuineness of what has been transmitted to you. In so far as these sessions are concerned you have given expression in substance to my thoughts with 100% accuracy. The wording you used is, of course, a matter of your own style; far be it from me to be critical of that!

So I'm glad to be able to confirm to you your feeling that you're being true to yourself - which is all any soul can hope to be. You need have no doubts about sharing with others either these sessions or your other counselling work. They are honest expressions of our truth (I, of course, include your guides in the "our"). What others take from them is their affair and their responsibility – and, if I may presume to say, their opportunity.

REINCARNATION – IV

19th – 23rd July: A particular phenomenon you have encountered in your counselling work is the fascination some people who believe in reincarnation have with discovering details of past lives and past relationships. This is something which bothers you as you feel that concentration to an immoderate degree on the past can only be detrimental to living in the present.

As we have seen in an earlier session, souls tend to reincarnate in groups. The sizes of groups vary; in human terms they are usually quite large, often running into millions. Within the groups there are sub-groups which for many reasons have chosen to operate contrasting interrelationships in different earth lives. For example, souls may choose to have roles as husbands and wives in contrasting sexual relationships in a number of lifetimes, or they may choose to be brothers or sisters, or parents and children. It all depends on what they want to learn in a lifetime; the souls with whom they choose to interrelate are those who they feel can best help them with their life purpose, and vice versa.

As I have already explained, the reason why souls don't generally remember their previous lives on earth is in order to allow them to have a fresh start without the burden (of guilt, etc.) which remembrance would place on them. At the same time the present can be helped by the past. For example, if a person is having problems with a particular relationship it can be helpful to him to know how those problems originated and to realise that part of his life purpose is to overcome the problems by mental adjustment to them within the restrictive earth setting. Or if a person has an obsessive interest in sex, or gambling, or eating, or alcohol, or anything at all, it can be beneficial to get to the source of the obsession; this is something which cannot be done by traditional methods, such as psychiatry, unless the obsession originated in the present lifetime, which is most unlikely.

The key to helpfulness, in my view, is selectivity in the presentation of experiences, both in the manner of presentation as well as in the experiences themselves. This can best be done by a medium or counsellor (or psychiatrist!) working under the guidance of evolved souls. In that way the person enjoys the possibility of understanding and accepting through knowledge without having to undergo the trauma of remembrance. Also the evolved souls will make sure that only information which will be of help to him in his present situation will be passed on to him; in other words, idle curiosity will not be satisfied in a purposeless way.

So the thing to do, I suggest, is to let what comes come and transmit it as best you can. You can neither control nor guarantee the effects..

STYLE

23rd July: Given that each soul is unique and has its own special place in the cosmic scheme of things, what is it that gives it its uniqueness?

If one observes any gathering of people it is possible straightaway to see that no two of them look exactly the same unless there are identical twins in the gathering. Even with identical twins acquaintance will reveal differences both in appearance and in qualities which distinguish one from the other.

On the human level there is - or should be - no difficulty about seeing the uniqueness of each person - although not alone in communities but in families acceptance of this uniqueness is often arrived at only after much misunderstanding and suffering. There are all sorts of physical differences as well as mental and temperamental ones which are usually obvious.

On the spiritual level the differences are not always so obvious.
Essentially they come into the area of awareness and its different stages.

I have said that each soul retains its individuality at the ultimate stage of full awareness while at the same time forming a unity with all other souls. What are the constituents of individuality in the ultimate sense?

I can encapsulate my answer in one word – style. By style I mean way of feeling and thinking and of expressing those feelings and thoughts.

One of the big problems on the human scene is that so much time is devoted to knocking the style out of individuals, that is, their own style, and making them conform to somebody else's. As awareness grows the development, or I should say the expression, of individual style is encouraged until ultimately there's no barrier to its expression.

Perhaps the simplest answer I can give to the question I posed at the beginning is that uniqueness is a matter of style which in the end comes down to being oneself without constraint of any kind.

CONCLUSION

Now we have reached the end of this book. To all those who read it – and to all those who don't – I wish joy and happiness and a speedy return to full awareness.

ABOUT THE AUTHOR

Paddy McMahon was born in 1933 in County Clare in the west of Ireland, and has lived in Dublin since 1952. Employed in the Irish Civil Service from 1952 until 1988, he became aware that he and all people had spirit guides-guardian angels, and that we can communicate with them if we so choose. These communications began in 1978, and inspired him to become increasingly involved in spiritual counseling and lecturing. Paddy's first communications from the highly-evolved spiritual being Shebaka began in 1981.

BOOKS BY PADDY MCMAHON

There Are No Goodbyes:
Guided By Angels - My Tour of the Spirit World

Peacemonger:
More Dialogue with Margaret Anna Cusack

Living without Fear:
Dialogue with J. Krishnamurti

Amongst Equals:
More Dialogue with J. Krishnamurti

A Free Spirit:
Dialogue with Margaret Anna Cusack The Nun of Kenmare

The Joy of Being
Illustrations by Michel

The Grand Design:
Reflections of a soul / oversoul
Selected excerpts from the five volumes

The Grand Design – V:
Reflections of a soul / oversoul

The Grand Design – IV:
Reflections of a soul / oversoul

The Grand Design – III:
Reflections of a soul / oversoul

The Grand Design – II:
Reflections of a soul / oversoul

The Grand Design – I:
Reflections of a soul / oversoul

Printed in Great Britain
by Amazon

74436915R00071